BEYOND ACCESS

BEYOND ACCESS

Indigenizing Programs for Native American Student Success

Edited by Stephanie J. Waterman, Shelly C. Lowe, and Heather J. Shotton

Foreword by George S. McClellan

STERLING, VIRGINIA

Published by Stylus Publishing, LLC.
22883 Quicksilver Drive Sterling, Virginia 20166-2102

Library of Congress Cataloging-in-Publication Data
Names: Waterman, Stephanie J., 1957- editor of compilation. |
Lowe, Shelly C., editor of compilation. |
Shotton, Heather J., 1976- editor of compilation.
Title: Beyond access : indigenizing programs for Native American
student success / edited by Stephanie J. Waterman, Shelly C. Lowe, and
Heather J. Shotton; foreword by George S. McClellan.
Other titles: Indigenizing programs for Native American student success
Description: First edition. |
Sterling, Virginia : Stylus Publishing, LLC., [2018] |
Includes bibliographical references and index.
Identifiers: LCCN 2017040162 (print) |
LCCN 2018000137 (ebook) |
ISBN 9781620362891 (uPDF) |
ISBN 9781620362907 (ePUB, mobi) |
ISBN 9781620362877 (cloth : acid-free paper) |
ISBN 9781620362884 (pbk. : acid-free paper) |
ISBN 9781620362891 (library networkable e-edition) |
ISBN 9781620362907 (consumer e-edition)
Subjects: LCSH: Indians of North America--Education (Higher) |
Indians of North America--Education (Higher)--Alaska.
Classification: LCC E97 (ebook) |
LCC E97 .B48 2018 (print) |
DDC 378.1/98297--dc23
LC record available at https://lccn.loc.gov/2017040162

13-digit ISBN: 978-1-62036-287-7 (cloth)
13-digit ISBN: 978-1-62036-288-4 (paperback)
13-digit ISBN: 978-1-62036-289-1 (library networkable e-edition)
13-digit ISBN: 978-1-62036-290-7 (consumer e-edition)

Printed in the United States of America

All first editions printed on acid-free paper
that meets the American National Standards Institute
Z39-48 Standard.

Bulk Purchases
Quantity discounts are available for use in workshops
and for staff development.
Call 1-800-232-0223

First Edition, 2018

To Arthur Taylor (Nez Perce) and Danielle Terrance (Mohawk), our relatives gone too soon.

And to all who create and support positive college-going experiences for Native and Indigenous students.

CONTENTS

BLESSING

Luci Tapahonso (Diné)

Diyin Dine'é, Holy Ones, Creator, the Sacred,

These voices/words are assembled in gratitude for the teachings
and stories of our ancestors, and the vast land granted them.
Our voices range from the Onondaga, Diné, the Cheyenne
and Arapaho, Lumbee as well as the Pueblo, Chippewa, Oglala Lakota,
Comanche and Apache Nations.
We are grateful for the contributors and their devotion to the future
of indigenous students, their children and the generations to follow.

We begin by acknowledging Nahaszáán, our mother the earth,
and all the sacred aspects of the pinon, sage or cedar smoke
which often accompany our songs and prayers.
We recall, and rejoice in, the refreshing female rains, urgent male rain,
silent new snowfall, lightning and thunder.

We are grateful for the bodies of waters that sustain us
year after year, generation after generation. We acknowledge
the timeless mountains throughout this land; their enduring
presence gives us strength to pursue our life's work.

We offer prayers for the continuing threats
to Nahaszáán, our mother the earth.

Diyin Dine'é, may we recall the optimism with which
we originally pursued our studies so we may
instill confidence and courage in students and colleagues.
May our classrooms, offices, and institutions exist as lively centers
of sound scholarship, new discoveries, and enduring wisdom.

Diyiin Diné, Creator, we are grateful for tasks
that demand our best effort, and for rewarding work

that honors our families and kin.

Holy Ones, help us to remember that an occasional failure
is not a measure of our worth, and that each season is a new beginning.
Help us to remember to share our stories and toils with one another
for it is only through stories that we live full lives.

Creator, help us to remember that we are surrounded
by blessings, seen and unseen.

May we always cherish our ancestors as we prepare for the days ahead;
their teachings can encourage us in times of uncertainty and instability.
We understand that we exist because of their prayers and faith.

Help us to remember to imbue each day with the kindness, humor
and compassion that distinguishes our indigenous traditions.

May these words, and our work, reflect the wisdom and optimism
that have sustained our forbearers for generations.

Hózhó nááhasdłíí'.
Hózhó nááhasdłíí'.
Hózhó nááhasdłíí'.
Hózhó nááhasdłíí'.
We are restored in beauty.

FOREWORD

A number of years ago, Shelly Lowe and I were copresenting in Albuquerque, New Mexico, at a meeting of the Southwest Sociological Association. We were sharing our respective doctoral research projects, both of which related to supporting the success of Native American students. As budding qualitative researchers, we began our presentation by dutifully sharing some of our own life experiences as a way of explaining how they might have shaped our work. The audience, including a number of Native American students, practitioners, and scholars, politely indulged us in this endeavor as young scholars. Shelly shared her story as a Navajo woman, student, and student affairs professional, and the audience nodded in understanding and appreciation. I began to share my experience as a European American male student affairs professional, noting that I had come up in the business through res life. A number of audience members were clearly puzzled, and I turned to Shelly looking for her thoughts. She gently pointed out to me that res life in my world (residential life) meant something completely different than rez life (life on the reservation) for members of our audience. Sometimes even when you come with a good heart and a clear mind, you cannot help but trip over your own cultural biases and limitations. In those moments, it is good to have a friend or a group of friends who can lead you to a richer and better understanding and share in the learning and laughter with you.

Vine Deloria (1991) once observed, "The thing that has always been missing in Indian education, and is still missing, is Indians" (p. 13). One of the many blessings that have come for me through more than 30 years of serving students in higher education is the opportunity to have seen a meaningful change in this regard when it comes to higher education. Over the past decade or so, an active and engaged network of Native practitioners and scholars has emerged, ensuring that Native voices are leading much-needed conversations about supporting the success of Native people—students, staff, and faculty in higher education. Their voices are in the forefront in meetings on campuses, presentations in academic and professional associations, programs of research and assessment, and scholarly publications.

Grounding their work in Indigenous theory and focusing on cultural assets and resilience, these practitioners and scholars work to problematize perceptions, programs, and policies reflecting deep misunderstandings and

profound ignorance about the sociohistorical context of the Native experience in European American education (including higher education), sovereignty and its implications for working with Native people, theories or
models of Native epistemology or identity, and knowledge about Native people today. These colleagues refer to their efforts as Indigenizing an environment, whether that environment is a campus, an association, or a publishing
opportunity. They offer insights into developing culturally appropriate and
responsive curriculum and programs reflecting the important values of
respect, relevance, reciprocity, and responsibility (Kirkness & Barnhardt,
1991). In addition, and perhaps most important, they offer mentorship and
role models to future Native American students, practitioners, and scholars.

In 2005, Mary Jo Tippeconnic Fox, Shelly Lowe, and I had the opportunity to edit a first-of-its-kind monograph focused exclusively on supporting
the success of Native American students in higher education. *Serving Native
American Students*, part of the New Directions in Student Services monograph series, was accepted for publication as the summer edition—a spot
typically reserved for works that are seen as focusing on important topics
that may have a limited appeal with regard to readership. The monograph
featured chapters contributed by a diverse array of Native American practitioners and scholars, and it proved immensely popular, with sales exceeding
all expectations and with much of the sales being attributed to single-copy
sales (purchases by those who do not subscribe to the monograph series).

It is my belief and hope that the monograph helped the publishing world
take note of both the availability of Native authors and the market for work
focused on Native American higher education. Since its publication, a number of outstanding works have been published in this area. *Native American
Higher Education in the United States* was revised in 2007. *American Indian
Higher Educational Experiences: Cultural Visions and Personal Journeys* was
published in 2008. In 2012, *Postsecondary Education for American Indian and
Alaskan Natives: Higher Education for Nation Building and Self-Determination*
was published as part of the ASHE Higher Education Report series. *Beyond
the Asterisk: Understanding Native Students in Higher Education* was published
in 2013, and *Indigenous Leadership in Higher Education* appeared in 2014.

*Beyond Access: Indigenizing Programs for Native American Student Suc-
cess* is another important work in this new body of Indigenous scholarship.
Heather J. Shotton, Shelly C. Lowe, and Stephanie J. Waterman, who have
been and continue to be among the group of leaders I mentioned earlier,
have once again assembled an impressive group of contributing authors.
Members of both tribes and campus communities from across the country,
the authors report on model programs designed to support the success of
Native American students in undergraduate and graduate majors in a variety

of institutional settings. One can clearly see that these programs are framed in Indigenous ways of knowing and being, and the four Rs—respect, relevance, reciprocity, and responsibility (Kirkness & Barnhardt, 1991)—are in clear evidence throughout all of them.

Having had the opportunity to share the journey of this change from some of the earliest meetings and conversations about what needed to be done and how that work could be pursued, it has been an incredible learning opportunity. I have joked with my friends and colleagues among this amazing group (both contributors to *Beyond Access* and many others) that if I could sing even the least little bit I would gladly offer an honor song for their accomplishments. My hope is that they will receive these words of introduction and appreciation as a more pleasing (and less painful) way of paying respect to their worthwhile contributions to the chorus of powerful Native voices now being heard on issues in Indian higher education.

George S. McClellan
Associate Professor of Higher Education
University of Mississippi

References

Brayboy, B. M. J., Fann, A. J., Castagno, A. E., & Solyom, J. A. (2012). Postsecondary education for American Indian and Alaska Natives: Higher education for nation building and self-determination. *ASHE Higher Education Report, 37*(5).

Carney, C. M. (2007). *Native American higher education* (2nd ed.). Piscataway, NJ: Transaction Publishers.

Deloria, V. (1991, Spring). The perpetual education report. *Winds of Change*, pp. 12–18. In M. J. T. Fox, S. C. Lowe, & G. S. McClellan (Eds.), *New directions for student services, serving Native American students* (no. 109, pp. 12–18). San Francisco, CA: Jossey-Bass.

Huffman, T. (2008). *American Indian higher educational experiences: Cultural visions and personal journeys.* New York, NY: Peter Lang Publishing.

Kirkness, V. J., & Barnhardt, R. (1991, May). First Nations and higher education: The four Rs—respect, relevance, reciprocity, responsibility. *Journal of American Indian Education.* Retrieved from http://jaie.asu.edu/v30/V30S3fir.htm

Minthorn, R., & Chavez, A. F. (2014). *Indigenous leadership in higher education.* New York, NY: Routledge.

Shotton, H., Lowe, S. C., & Waterman, S. J. (Eds.). (2013). *Beyond the asterisk: Understanding native students in higher education.* Sterling, VA: Stylus.

INTRODUCTION

*Stephanie J. Waterman (Onondaga), Heather J. Shotton
(Wichita/Kiowa/Cheyenne), and Shelly C. Lowe (Diné)*

*You aren't going nowhere. You're not going to do anything.
You'll still be in this neighborhood 20 years from now.*

(Non-Native eleventh-grade teacher)

Indians don't go to college.

(Non-Native high school guidance counselor)

The previous are direct quotes from Native American participants in a study on degree completion (Waterman, 2004, 2007). The participants quoted went to different high schools five years apart: one in the city of Buffalo, New York, and the other near the Mohawk Nation in northern New York. Clearly, these participants were not seen as college material by the very people who should have been assisting students with educational goals. As Indigenous scholars and professionals, we often hear our colleagues make blanket statements about our students, such as, "Native families don't want their children to go to college" or "Native students don't want to leave home and that's why they don't go to college." These few examples indicate that the deficit model is still alive and well. If these are the common perceptions educational professionals have of Indigenous students, then how are our students finding their way to college? How do our students create pathways to college?

Neither student quoted came from a schooling environment that "normalized" college-going in order to produce a "college culture" in their high school. Jarsky, McDonough, and Nuñez (2002) name key factors for creating such a culture. These factors include having clear educational and college expectations, providing a college-preparatory curriculum, providing access to college application processes, supporting access to the ACT and/or SAT, and offering strong college counseling. Additionally, we argue the importance and need for Native and community role models, along with culturally

1

appropriate and meaningful support avenues. Native communities clearly value education. The majority of our students have been told throughout their lives that education is "a ladder," a "weapon," a tool their communities need to combat historical atrocities and identify and create solutions to the challenges facing their tribal nations. Education is also seen as a pathway to cultural revitalization and sustainability; it is a critical part of nation building for our tribal nations. The encouragement to seek higher education is often given with statements such as, "Go to college, get your degree, then come back home and help us."

Although we encourage college education as a form of nation building, the scholarship has yet to explore the ways that Indigenous students, communities, and tribal nations are creating pathways to college. In this book, we highlight Indigenized college access programs. By Indigenized we mean programs developed *by*, not just *for*, the Indigenous community. Indigenized programs value approaches that privilege Indigenous values, knowledge, and perspectives. We argue that widely embraced college-going environments often fail because they are normalized—normalized to the dominant, mainstream educational system that has been used as a tool for the elimination of Indigenous culture, language, and community. The boarding school era was a brutal system sponsored by churches and the federal government to replace Native cultural with another (Wright, 1988). Mainstream educational systems in the Americas are based on Eurocentric values such as individualism, Christianity, paternalism, competitiveness, and nuclear family systems, which are often incompatible with Indigenous value systems of community, sharing, extended family systems, giving back to one's community, and a respect for creation as a relation not as a resource (Deloria & Wildcat, 2001). Institutions of higher education were developed for and by a particular class of White men, primarily to provide avenues into the clergy and train leaders for their communities (Lucas, 2006). The system was brought with the colonizers from across Europe and has been steadily influenced by European values in its development (Rudolph, 1990). It has historically benefited the White, male, and wealthy class. Our postsecondary system today is a product of that structure, and we interpret current resistance to diversity and ethnic studies as remnants of an organization based on male privilege and the maintenance of a status quo.

. Native students are also a product of their environments. Although many of our Indigenous communities—urban, rural, and suburban—struggle to maintain their traditions while simultaneously confronting poverty, stereotypes, poor schools, and competitive schooling environments (Brayboy, Fann, Castagno, & Solyom, 2012), a high value is placed on the desire to use traditional values to influence our youth and communities. Even Indigenous students who attend competitive K–20 systems struggle to balance their Indigenous ways of being within the schooling environment. During the Q&A portion of a presentation on our first book, the mother of a college student shared a comment about her son's recruitment experience with the Massachusetts Institute of Technology (MIT). MIT's tuition is very high, but academically successful engineering students can earn high salaries, and a particular MIT admissions representative stressed the potential income as a solution to the high tuition cost. However, this Mohawk student wanted to return to his community with his engineering degree to work for his people, an environment that could not provide the income to repay the MIT tuition. For many Native students, gaining an education to "get ahead" is not a common reason given for going to college.

Brayboy and colleagues (2012) write, "individual development happens for the betterment of the community" (p. 16) rather than individual status. Yet higher education institutions tend to emphasize individual gains such as personal income (Deil-Amen & Turley, 2007; Leonhardt, 2014). Nelson (2015) questions comparing these individual "outcomes" to Native students. The relationship between education and nation building is more than individual income and individual benefit, particularly when personal income for a college graduate working on a reservation will typically be much lower than off-reservation, even when employed with a professional degree in one's major.

Although building an independent economic base is important to tribal nation building, strengthening tribes' Indigenous knowledge systems, our diverse Native cultural capital, and exercising our sovereignty are at its foundation. Brayboy and colleagues (2012) write, "Ultimately, for us, the process of nation building consists of legal and political, cultural, economic, health and nutrition, spiritual, and education elements with the well-being, sovereignty, self-determination, and autonomy of the community as the driving force for nation building" (p. 13). Alfred (2005) uses the term *strengthening* in his definition of *nation building*. Nation building necessarily requires higher education (Brayboy et al., 2012). Much of access to higher education, which we focus on in this book, comes out of tribal assessments of needs based on geographical location, economic (in)stability, health profiles, natural resource responsibilities, language revitalization, cultural management, and other aspects related to their inherent sovereignty and rights as distinct tribal nations. Access programs, more often than not, arise out of a tribe's needs for skilled tribal citizens with the educational knowledge provided in institutions of higher education. Tribes need educated citizens with the skills and capacity to address and problem solve their most basic challenges.

The programs in this text are examples of exercising our sovereignty to educate and support students, incorporating Indigenous knowledge systems in ways that enable our students to access a college education to return to their communities and strengthen their nation's infrastructure. A deep sense of reciprocity or giving back to one's community is a consistent theme in Indigenous college student literature (Brayboy, Castagno, & Solyom, 2014; J. P. Guillory, 2008; R. M. Guillory, 2009; Lee, 2009; Shotton, Oosahwe, & Cintrón, 2007). Related to content relevance (Kirkness & Barnhart, 1991) students seek a college education to improve their communities and are academically more successful when the material is relevant to Indigenous student experiences. Although tribes and Native higher education professionals have worked diligently to create culturally relevant access programs, in some instances institutions of higher education have taken the lead in identifying and creating access avenues for Native students. Both federal and state governments have done the same by earmarking funding to provide tribal entities the financial incentive to create programs and support students in high-need areas such as science, technology, engineering, and mathematics (STEM).

In discussing possible titles for our book, the word "pathways" appeared in many drafts. The pathway image seemed fitting because it reflects diverse types of paths: pressed earth, well-worn, flattened grass, plank, and so on; accounts for gait: fast walkers, those who saunter, and everything in between; includes varying directions, starts and stops; and consists of different types of markers, descriptors, or warnings. Paths are rarely straight. Imagine walking in freshly fallen snow, thinking you had walked straight to your destination. Upon looking back, your footsteps steadily made progress to your destination but not in a straight line, and each step may not appear well defined. As the stories in this book reflect, access to higher education pathways move toward a goal: some paths are straight, many are not, but providing support on that pathway to reach the end goal is essential.

This book is a follow-up to *Beyond the Asterisk: Understanding Native Students in Higher Education* (Shotton, Waterman, & Lowe, 2013), in which we provided readers, both Native and non-Native, with information on the unique and often assumed experiences of Indigenous students, faculty, staff, and administrators in U.S. institutions of higher education. Our hope in *Beyond the Asterisk* was to push beyond issues of invisibility of Natives in higher education to foster a better understanding of how to create meaningful and culturally supportive environments that promote acceptance, encouragement, and success for Native students, who even to this day continue to be overlooked in many Non-Native Colleges and Universities (NNCUs). For example, in Chapter 2 of *Beyond the Asterisk*, "Incorporating Native Culture in Student Affairs," Steven C. Martin (Muscogee Creek) and Adrienne L. Thunder (Ho-Chunk) emphasized that our job is to support students in postsecondary environments. To help Native students to succeed, we need to provide them with what they need for growth, and supporting their cultural identity is key. They wrote, "To have the elements needed for their continued growth, a familiar content with rules for participation that Native students recognize and understand, including a sense that they are important, valued members of their campus community is also necessary" (Martin & Thunder, 2013, p. 42). In Chapter 3, "Extending the Rafters: Cultural Context for Native Students," Timothy Ecklund and the late Danielle Terrance (Mohawk) shared how Haudenosaunee Longhouse concepts were used in the development of a living learning unit. In this book, we hope to again push beyond current understandings about Natives and college access and highlight Indigenized approaches to creating pathways to college. *Beyond the Asterisk*, like this book, is not meant to be the definitive guide. Instead, both books are meant to create dialogue and serve as starting points for additional research, examination, and publications.

Definition of Terms

Throughout this book, as we did in *Beyond the Asterisk*, we use various terminologies that we feel are important to define for our readers. There are 567 federally recognized tribes within the borders of what is now called the United States. The U.S. government uses the term *American Indian/Alaska Native* to represent the racial classification of individuals who are members of these tribes. The U.S. government also identifies Native Hawaiians as a racial category for individuals whose Indigenous ancestry originates from Hawaii. We acknowledge that we were not able to include our Native Hawaiian kin in the current book, but we do not want to exclude them in our definitions. How an Indigenous person identifies is diverse. In certain parts of the Americas, *American Indian* is preferred, whereas in other parts, *Native American* or just *Native* is used. *Indigenous* is often used in a more political sense, and our brothers and sisters north of the imposed U.S.–Canadian border use *First Nations, Aboriginal, Métis*, and *Inuit*. However, we almost all prefer to identify with our tribal community or communities: Onondaga, Diné, Wichita/Kiowa/Cheyenne. In this book, we use many terms because the diverse Native American community uses many terms. Some Indigenous communities live on territories, whereas others on reservations, and many use the term *tribe* and others, *nations*. We do not want to further colonize by imposing a single term for our diverse people. We recommend that when you work with an Indigenous population, ask the community you're working with about their preferred terminology.

American Indian/Native American/Native/Indigenous

The terms *American Indian*, *Native American*, *Native*, and *Indigenous* are all used interchangeably throughout this book. Each of these terms refers to the Indigenous populations of North America, particularly those located in what we now know as the United States, and those who identify as Native American or Alaska Native. This includes those who are members or descendants of both federally and state recognized tribes and Alaska Native corporations. Native people are both political and racialized beings (Brayboy, 2005). It is important to understand that Native people are not just an ethnic minority. Rather our identity is situated within our unique status as members of sovereign nations; hence, we are also recognized as a political group. Often this political status exists in two countries, such as with the United States and Mexico or with the United States and Canada. These international borders were imposed on tribal territories by colonial systems, which can affect tribal membership status due to country of citizenship, but are generally not a factor in how one conceives of one's individual tribal identity. Although this book does not focus on Native Hawaiian students and communities, we acknowledge our Native Hawaiian brothers and sisters and assert that our populations face many similar challenges in higher education. We stress that future work is needed to understand both the unique issues of access for Native Hawaiian students and Hawaiian-specific approaches to college pathways, as well as work that honors and includes multiple Indigenous perspectives.

Indian Country

When discussing Native populations, it is important to understand where Native people actually reside. The issue of Native land and residential patterns is complex and tied to our histories with federal governments and policies of removal, allotment, and relocation (Shotton, 2016). The U.S. Census (2010) American Indian/Alaska Native–specified areas include federal reservations as well as state reservations, off-reservation trust land, and Alaska Native, state, and tribal statistical areas. Native people populate different areas of the United States, Canada, and Mexico, and it is important to understand that Natives reside on reservations or reserves, reservation/reserve border towns, rural communities, territories, and urban areas alike (Shotton, Lowe, & Waterman, 2013). *Indian Country* is then defined to encompass all these territories and areas.

Native American–Serving Nontribal Institutions

Native American–Serving Nontribal Institutions (NASNTI) are institutions of higher education that have a Native American undergraduate student enrollment of at least 10% and are not a Tribal College or University (White House Initiative on American Indian/Alaska Native Education, n.d.). NASNTIs are authorized under Title III, Parts A and F of the Higher Education Act, which provides grants and related assistance to enable these institutions to improve and expand their capacity to serve Native Americans (U.S. Department of Education, n.d.).

Non-Native Colleges and Universities

We continue to use the term *NNCUs* to describe those institutions that represent the predominantly White population, typically referred to as predominantly White institutions or mainstream institutions. The use of the term *NNCU* is a conscious effort to center our experience as Native people (Shotton, Waterman, & Lowe, 2013).

Tribal Colleges and Universities

The terms *tribal colleges* and *tribal colleges and universities* (TCUs) are used interchangeably throughout this book. TCU refers to those colleges and universities chartered by tribal governments. Tribal identity is the core of every TCU, and they all share the mission of tribal self-determination and service to their respective communities.

Tribal Education Agency

The term *tribal educational agency* means an authorized governmental agency of an American Indian tribe, an Alaska Native tribe, or tribal organization (as defined in the Indian Self-Determination and Education Assistance Act, 25 U.S.C 450b) that is primarily responsible for regulating, administering, or supervising the formal education of tribal members. *Tribal educational agency* includes tribal education departments, tribal divisions of education, tribally sanctioned educational authorities, tribal education administrative planning and development agencies, tribal education agencies, tribal administrative education entities, and Alaska Native corporations operating education programs for Alaska Native students (National Indian Education Association, n.d.).

College Access

Because of the Higher Education Act of 1965's emphasis on grants to institutions to increase access to individuals who could not afford college (Higher Education Act of 1965), access has historically been discussed through financial aid as a means to enhance admission. Access, however, is more than access to financial aid or admission to an institution. Students need access to information such as financial aid and how to navigate the financial aid process, college preparation coursework, ACT and SAT prep courses, study skills, and skills such as how to talk to a professor and find support on campus. Access is often narrowly discussed in the literature and by the public in ways that are ahistorical so as not to problematize the structure of higher education, a structure that needed legislation and subsequent policies to expand access.

Limited Literature

We know that Native students remain one of the most underrepresented groups in higher education (Snyder & Dillow, 2015). Scholars have discussed at length the obstacles that Native students face once they get into college (see Huffman, 2010). In more recent years, scholars have moved the discussion about Natives in higher education to one of nation building, strength, and success (Brayboy, Castagno, & Solyom, 2014; Brayboy et al., 2012; J. P. Guillory, 2008; Kirkness & Barnhardt, 1991; Lee, 2009; Minthorn & Chavez, 2015; Shotton, Lowe, & Waterman, 2013). But our knowledge about college access, particularly the ways in which Native students and communities are creating pathways to college, is limited.

Native Student Enrollment

In 2012, more than 14% of Native American high school students did not return in the fall semester or were enrolled in an alternative program (Stark & Noel, 2015). Based on 2013 data, the completion rate of those who remained in high school was 82%, and yet the college degree completion rate was only 14% (Snyder & Dillow, 2015). Bureau of Indian Education schools reported a dismal high school graduation rate of 53% (Executive Office of the President, 2014). For context, in the same time period, the high school completion rate for White students was 93%, 76% for Black students, and 66% for Latino/a students. However, more Native students reported a desire to earn a bachelor's degree in 2012 than in 2006 (Snyder & Dillow, 2015). Native students make up 0.8% of the total college student population (National Center for Education Statistics, 2014), and 4% reported taking a remedial course in their first year of college (Snyder & Dillow, 2015).

Native American students often attend poorly resourced secondary schools that are unable to offer the math and sciences necessary to prepare them for postsecondary education. Rural and heavily populated urban schools are rarely funded on par with suburban schools and are populated by minoritized students, including Native students. Because of the lack of school resources, Native students are the least likely to enroll in Advanced Placement courses, and only one in four will take the ACT (Executive Office of the President, 2014). Taking the ACT or SAT is an important component of college access. The College Board reported that 79% of students who took the SAT in 2010 enrolled in a postsecondary institution by 2011 (McKillip & Mackey, 2013). Access to WiFi is still a problem for remote schools and communities.

Similar to other groups, Native American women enroll in higher education at a higher rate than men, and students with a parent who earned a degree were more likely to complete a four-year degree (McKillip & Mackey, 2013). Yet many of the schools that our students attend do not offer entrance exam preparatory classes, and, as will be shared in our book, access programs recognize this gap and step in to offer these services.

Native Americans earned 0.5% of all master's degrees in 2013 (National Center for Education Statistics, 2015). At this level, women are earning more degrees than men; however, the gap is greater because 65% of these degrees are earned by Native women. These degrees are typically in the disciplines of social services and business. Of all doctorates earned in 2013, Native Americans earned 0.4% in similar social service fields noted previously, and women are still earning 61% of these advanced degrees (National Center for Education Statistics, 2015). Disparities abound for women and people of color in the STEM fields (National Science Board, 2016). For Native Americans, the disparities are even more glaring. Of all degrees earned by Native Americans in 2012, only 14% were in STEM, and at the master's level, only 8%. Of the 231 doctoral degrees awarded to Native Americans in 2012, 107 were in STEM. However, in the STEM disciplines, we see a gender reversal: Native men earned 55% of bachelor's degrees, 58% of master's degrees, and 73% of doctorate degrees.

An area with even higher disparities for Native Americans is nursing. Although the U.S. Department of Health and Human Services' Health Resources and Services Administration (2013) states, "The number of individuals pursuing nursing education has increased in recent years," the American Association of Colleges of Nursing (2015) identifies the need to attract students from American Indian and Alaska Native backgrounds as a high priority for the nursing profession. Although we see nationally the number of American Indian/Alaska Native students in all nursing programs reported at 1.0% (National League for Nursing, 2013), a closer look at the numbers shows a slight decline between 2009 and 2014 in the total percentage of American Indian/Alaska Native students enrolled in entry-level baccalaureate, master's, and doctoral nursing programs (American Association of Colleges of Nursing, 2013).

Before we continue, we need to discuss the problem with data and racial terminology. As noted in previous work (Garland, 2007; Shotton, Lowe, & Waterman, 2013), data, research, and literature are lacking because of the "American Indian research asterisk" (Garland, 2007, p. 622). Due to low populations enrolled, statistical analysis is problematic; hence, we are often omitted from national and institutional reports. For example, with regard to American Indian/Alaska Native students, the National Center for Education Statistics (2014) recent report on high school dropout and completion rates cautions that, because of small sample size, "reliable trend analysis could not be conducted" (p. 6) and a high standard error occurs. Beginning in 2011, student data collected with new racial identification options showed a decrease in the numbers of American Indian/Alaska Native–identified students enrolled in postsecondary education each year, whereas the numbers of students who identified with two or more races increased each year (National Center for Education Statistics, 2014). The small sample size "problem" that excludes Native students in national studies has only been exacerbated with increased racial identification categories and reporting options, which have literally begun to erase American Indian–identified students in national data.

Organization of the Book

In the majority of mainstream educational environments, Indigenous students must adapt to the educational program. The President's 2014 Executive Report on Native Youth concluded that a "root cause" of Indigenous gaps in K–12 educational attainment is due to the lack of tribal control (Executive Office of the President, 2014). As we have discussed, such programs are often ill fitting and privilege dominant, Western culture and values. In this book, we have chosen to privilege Indigenous knowledge, culture, and values by featuring college access approaches that have adapted, or developed from scratch, programs for the unique Indigenous populations they serve. As Native individuals, we begin this book in the way we were taught to begin all important tasks: with a blessing by our own mentor and scholar, Luci Tapahonso (Diné). Beginning in this way is a sharing of our good intentions for the work we do and the work our readers will continue.

In Chapter 1, we begin with Natalie Youngbull's (Southern Cheyenne and Arapaho, Ft. Peck Sioux and Assiniboine) personal story. Her chapter provides the voice of one who has benefited from college access programs all the way to her doctoral program. She shares her experiences in the Colorado University Upward Bound program and the Tribal Resources in Business, Engineering, and Science program at the University of New Mexico. She also writes about being a Gates Millennium Scholar and her own research on Gates scholars. She writes, "My successes in higher education would not have been realized without these college prep programs."

Throughout this book, we have incorporated narratives from current Indigenous graduate students. As we work to privilege Indigenous approaches to college access, we felt it was important to honor the place of story for Indigenous people. As Indigenous people, stories play a central role in our tribal communities; as Indigenous scholars, they play a central role in our work. In her discussion of storywork as a methodological approach, Jo-Ann Archibald (Stol:lo) (2008) asserts, the "power and beauty of stories is to educate and heal our people" (p. 371). In that belief in the power of story, we have woven stories of Indigenous graduate students into this book.

The students discuss the influence of their communities and tribal values on their college journeys. Breanna Faris (Cheyenne and Arapaho) explains, "Although academic resources and programs are critical in retention efforts, my greatest resource has always been my people." Monty Begaye (Diné) talks of his desire to help other Native students: "My college journey changed to a venture of how I could help create access and opportunities in higher education for students who may come from a similar disadvantaged background as mine." Writing about leadership, Cory Still (Cherokee), a current doctoral student, says, "For me leadership is not something I ever really sought. It is something that emerged from me through my cultural teachings" (Still, 2015, p. 203). Nakay Flotte, a Lipan Apache doctoral student at Harvard, tells the story of his difficult path to and in higher education: "My mind was bombarded by questions influenced by gender, class, race, and social etiquette: how should I approach a *madgani* stranger, who could I ask for help, how do I learn to study, and how do I handle everyday racism?" The students write about the interconnection of family, community, and spirituality—the foundations on which they heavily relied—along with the support they received from fellow students, faculty, and programs, which helped them find meaning in their higher education pursuits.

In Chapter 2, Adrienne Keene (Cherokee) provides an intimate look at the college application journey of two Native American high school students who participated in the College Horizons program. This program, which provides college admissions workshops to high school sophomore- and junior-level American Indian/Alaska Native and Native Hawaiian students across the United States, is founded on the premise that these bright and talented students do not receive quality college counseling and academic advising. The five-day "crash course," which is offered in partnership with a college or university, provides personal and culturally minded mentoring by higher education admissions officers, tribal community experts, and Native higher education professionals.

Chapter 3 discusses the role that TCUs play in college access for Native students. Matthew Makomenaw (Grand Traverse Bay Band of Ottawa and Chippewa Indians) and David Sanders (Oglala Sioux) highlight the key role of TCUs, which are designed to empower tribal communities and provide college access where little higher educational opportunity exists, while also highlighting the need for more data and research.

In Chapter 4, Christine Nelson (Diné and Laguna Pueblo) and Amanda Tachine (Diné) challenge the myth that Native American students attend college for free. They argue that financial aid for today's Native student is entangled within a historical and political context that is relevant to their current experience. By framing financial aid and a higher education system that was designed to assimilate Native Americans, they complicate these systems and discuss the role of Native nation building.

In Chapter 5, Lee Bitsóí (Diné) and Shelly C. Lowe (Diné) examine current effective practices in recruiting and retaining Native American students who are interested in pursuing careers in the STEM disciplines. An overview of funding that has greatly impacted the number of Native students entering STEM programs is provided, along with an introduction to professional organizations supporting these students. Included in the examination is an analysis of leading colleges and universities, including TCUs, that graduate the highest number of Native American students in STEM programs. Last, plausible prescriptions of common successful recruitment and retention strategies are provided for higher education campus educators.

Chapter 6 provides an overview of the Recruitment and Retention of Alaskan Natives into Nursing (RRANN) program at the University of Alaska Anchorage School of Nursing. In this chapter, Tina DeLapp, Jackie Pflaum, and Stephanie Sanderlin (Yupik/Unangan) address the shortage of Alaska Native/American Indian nurses in Alaska and identify how RRANN has sought to incorporate and use as a foundation the Ten Universal Alaska Native Values to provide culturally appropriate avenues for student support.

In Chapter 7, Susan Faircloth (Coharie) and Robin Minthorn (Kiowa, Nez Perce, Umatilla, Assiniboine) discuss the evolution of educational leadership programs for Native students. They begin with a discussion of the emergence of programs aimed at preparing Native principals, superintendents, and other school leaders, and then they move into the development of more culturally relevant leadership programs.

In Chapter 8, John Garland (Choctaw) reports on the sparse data available regarding Native American college students with disabilities, presenting this chapter as a starting point for more research and conversation. Like non-Native populations, Native American college students with disabilities are increasing on our college campuses, and we need to know how ability status may be defined by tribes and what data are available. Garland offers recommendations to support our students.

In the conclusion, we summarize the themes from the book and provide a discussion of the sociocultural capital in relation to nation building. Then, to illustrate how a community might increase college access in their own schools, we discuss the Norman Public Schools College Links program. Finally, we close with recommendations.

References

Alexie, S. (1996). *The Lone Ranger and Tonto fistfight in heaven*. New York, NY: Harper

Alfred, G. T. (2005). *Wasáse: Indigenous pathways of action and freedom*. Peterborough, Ontario, Canada: Broadview Press.

American Association of Colleges of Nursing. (2013). *Race/ethnicity data on students enrolled in nursing programs: 10-year data on minority students in baccalaureate and graduate programs*. Retrieved from www.aacn.nche.edu/research-data/EthnicityTbl.pdf

American Association of Colleges of Nursing. (2015). *Fact sheet: Enhancing diversity in the nursing workforce*. Retrieved from www.aacn.nche.edu/media-relations/fact-sheets/enhancing-diversity

Archibald, J. (2008). An Indigenous storywork methodology. In J. G. Knowles & A. L. Cole (Eds.), *Handbook of the arts in qualitative research* (pp. 371–384). Thousand Oaks, CA: Sage.

Brayboy, B. M. J. (2005). Toward a tribal critical race theory in education. *The Urban Review, 37*(5), 425–446.

Brayboy, B. M. J., Castagno, A. E., & Solyom, J. A. (2014). Looking into the hearts of Native peoples: Nation building as an institutional orientation for graduate education. *American Journal of Education, 120*(4), 575–596.

Brayboy, B. M. J., Fann, A. J., Castagno, A. E., & Solyom, J. A. (2012). Postsecondary education for American Indian and Alaska Natives: Higher education for nation-building and self-determination. *ASHE Higher Education Report, 37*(5), 1–154.

Deil-Amen, R., & Turley, R. L. (2007). A review of the transition college literature in sociology. *Teachers College Record, 109*(10), 2324–2366.

Deloria, V., Jr., & Wildcat, D. R. (2001). *Power and place: Indian education in America*. Golden, CO: Fulcrum.

Executive Office of the President. (2014). *2014 Native youth report*. Washington DC: The White House.

Garland, J. L. (2007). [Review of the book *Serving Native American students: New directions for student services*, by M. J. Tippeconic Fox, Shelley C. Lowe, & George S. McClellan.] *Journal of College Student Development, 48*, 612–614.

Guillory, J. P. (2008). Diverse pathways of "giving back" to tribal community: Perceptions of Native American college graduates (Unpublished doctoral dissertation). Pullman, WA: Washington State University.

Guillory, R. M. (2009). American Indian/Alaskan Native college student retention strategies. *Journal of Development Education, 33*(2), 12–38.

Health Resources and Services Administration. (2013). *The U.S. nursing workforce: Trends in supply and education*. Retrieved from https://www.scribd.com/document/252930934/Nursing-Workforce

Higher Education Act of 1965. Retrieved from https://legcounsel.house.gov/Comps/Higher%20Education%20Act%20Of%201965.pdf

Huffman, T. (2010). *Theoretical perspectives on American Indian education: A new look at educational success and the achievement gap*. Lanham, MD: AltaMira Press.

Jarsky, K. M., McDonough, P. M., & Nuñez, A. (2002). Establishing a college culture in secondary schools through P-20 collaboration: A case study. *Journal of Hispanic Higher Education, 8*(4), 357–373.

Kirkness, V. J., & Barnhardt, R. (1991). First Nations and higher education: The four Rs—respect, relevance, reciprocity, responsibility. *Journal of American Indian Education, 30*(3), 1–15.

Lee, T. S. (2009). Building Native nations through Native students' commitment to their communities. *Journal of American Indian Education, 48*(1), 19–36.

Leonhardt, D. (2014, May 27). Is college worth it? Clearly, data say. *The New York Times*, Everyday Economics. Retrieved from www.nytimes.com/2014/05/27/upshot/is-college-worth-it-clearly-new-data-say.html?_r=0

Lucas, J. R. (2006). *American higher education: A history* (2nd ed.). Baltimore, MD: The Johns Hopkins University Press.

Martin, S. C., & Thunder, A. L. (2013). Incorporating Native culture into student affairs. In H. J. Shotton, S. C. Lowe, & S. J. Waterman (Eds.), *Beyond the asterisk: Understanding Native students in higher education* (pp. 39–51). Sterling, VA: Stylus.

McKillip, M. E. M., & Mackey, P. E. (2013). *College access and success among high school graduates taking the SAT: Native American Students. Research Note 2013-4.* New York, NY: The College Board.

Minthorn, R. S., & Chavez, A. F. (Eds.). (2015). *Indigenous leadership in higher education* (Vol. 3). New York, NY: Routledge.

National Center for Education Statistics. (2014). Total fall enrollment in degree-granting postsecondary institutions, by level of enrollment, sex, attendance status, and race/ethnicity of student: Selected years, 1976 through 2014. *Digest of Education Statistics*. Retrieved from https://nces.ed.gov/programs/digest/d15/tables/dt15_306.10.asp

National Center for Education Statistics. (2015). *Digest of education statistics, 2013* (NCES 2015-011), Institute of Education Sciences, U.S. Department of Education, Washington D.C. Retrieved from https://nces.ed.gov/fastfacts/display.asp?id=171

National Indian Education Association. (n.d.). *Strengthening tribal participation in education*. Retrieved from www.usetinc.org/wp-content/uploads/LizMalerba/WWS%20LnP/1_30_15/ESEA%20TEA%20Project%20One-pager.pdf

National League for Nursing. (2013). *Annual survey of schools of nursing, fall 2012.* Retrieved from www.nln.org.research/slides/index.htm

National Science Board. (2016). *Science and engineering indicators 2016.* Retrieved from www.nsf.gov/statistics/2016/nsb20161/#/

Nelson, C. A. (2015). *American Indian college students as Native nation-builders: Tribal financial aid as a lens for understanding college-going paradoxes* (Unpublished doctoral dissertation). Tucson, AZ: University of Arizona.

Rudolph, F. (1990). *The American college & university: A history.* Athens, GA: The University of Georgia Press.

Shotton, H. J. (2016). *Beyond reservations: Exploring diverse backgrounds and tribal citizenship among Native college students.* Commissioned by the Racial Heterogeneity Project: National Commission on Asian American & Pacific Islander Research in Education. Los Angeles, CA: UCLA Institute for Immigration, Globalization, and Education.

Shotton, H. J., Lowe, S. C., & Waterman, S. J. (Eds.). (2013). *Beyond the asterisk: Understanding Native students in higher education.* Sterling, VA: Stylus.

Shotton, H. J., Oosahwe, E. S. L., & Cintrón, R. (2007). Stories of success: Experiences of American Indian students in a peer-mentoring retention program. *Review of Higher Education, 31*(1), 81–107.

Snyder, T. D., & Dillow, S. A. (2015). *Digest of education statistics 2013* (NCES 2015-011). Washington DC: National Center for Education Statistics, Institute of Education Sciences, U.S. Department of Education.

Stark, P., & Noel, A. M. (2015). *Trends in high school dropout and completion rates in the United States: 1972-2012* (NCES 2015-015). Washington DC: National Center for Education Statistics, U.S. Department of Education. Retrieved from http://nces.ed.gov/pubsearch

Still, C. (2015). Path of a modern warrior: Leadership perspectives through cultural teachings. In R. S. Minthorn & A. F. Chávez (Eds.), *Indigenous leadership in higher education* (pp. 196–203). New York, NY: Routledge.

U.S. Census. (2010). *Geographic terms and concepts—American Indian, Alaska Native, and Native Hawaiian areas.* Retrieved from https://www.census.gov/geo/reference/gtc/gtc_aiannha.html

U.S. Department of Education. (n.d.). *Native American-serving non-tribal institutions program.* Retrieved from https://www2.ed.gov/programs/nasnti/index.html

Waterman, S. J. (2004). *The Haudenosaunee College experience: A complex path to degree completion* (Doctoral dissertation). Syracuse, NY: Syracuse University.

Waterman, S. J. (2007). A complex path to Haudenosaunee degree completion. *Journal of American Indian Education, 46*(1), 20–40.

White House Initiative on American Indian/Alaska Native Education. U. S. Department of Education. (n.d.). *NASNTIs.* Retrieved from https://sites.ed.gov/whiaiane/nasntis/

Wright, B. (1988). "For the children of the Infidels"? American Indian education in the colonial colleges. *American Indian Culture and Research Journal, 12*(3), 1–14.

BREANNA'S STORY

Breanna Faris (Cheyenne and Arapaho)

My name is Breanna Rose Faris, and I am Cheyenne and Arapaho from the Youngbear family of Watonga, Oklahoma. I am the daughter of Bernice Youngbear and Mike Faris, and the granddaughter of Blossom and Clinton Youngbear and Mary and John Faris. I am named after my great grandmother, Rosie Touching Ground. I am a daughter, granddaughter, niece, sister, cousin, auntie, and partner. I am also a student affairs professional and doctoral student at the University of Oklahoma (OU).

As a doctoral student, I recognize I would not be where I am today without those who helped me get here. Although academic resources and programs are critical in retention efforts, my greatest resource has always been my people. I could have gone down different paths at any time, but I always had the right people in my life at the right times. I want to honor those people by telling my story.

As a young child, my mother and father set high educational goals for me and my sisters. They challenged us each time we brought report cards home. "That's great! Next time see if you can beat your score. You can do it," my mother would say. My two older sisters, Kara and Theresa, also set examples for me and my younger sister, Rainey, to follow. While this foundation was laid, our family was whole. However, my parents divorced when I was in elementary school, and things changed drastically for our family.

After the long, ugly divorce process, my father left with Rainey, and Kara moved out. My mother worked constantly to provide for me and Theresa while trying to find herself after the divorce. She turned to alcohol, causing further devastation for me and my sisters. Fights, family deaths, and overwhelming negativity became commonplace. However, our love for each other never ceased, and learning to love and support our mother through her addiction is one of our greatest accomplishments as a family.

My sisters and I found ways to survive. Theresa worked long hours after school to help pay bills. Rainey came home, and we did the best we could to make sense of our world together. Theresa taught us how to take care of ourselves and how to balance work, school, and our family life. She remained an all-star athlete and student. She eventually became a Gates Millennium Scholar and was accepted to OU. Kara brought joy back into our family

17

by having her first child. This child, along with the others who followed, became the glue that held our family together.

Although many things were out of my control, I found comfort knowing I could control my educational journey. Because Theresa was a Gates Scholar, I went into high school knowing what it took to become one, and it became my ticket out. During high school, teachers, friends, and extended family supported me. My friends made sure I had a ride to school and work. They made sure I had a place to stay when I did not feel safe at home, but above all else, they listened. Teachers reminded me I was capable and deserving of a college education. Our Indian education counselor, who was also my auntie, made sure I completed my Gates application. She stayed up with me and proofread my application late into the night. Our tribal education programs helped me by providing athletic shoes, school supplies, and other resources. Because of this collective support from my community, I was awarded the Gates Millennium Scholarship and went to OU.

When I got there, I was overwhelmed and relieved. I was relieved to finally have my own home, and I was overwhelmed by the campus atmosphere of a predominantly non-Native institution. I also had a significant amount of guilt for leaving Rainey and the rest of my family. Theresa did not finish college and was back at home, but she made a place for me at OU. Students, faculty, and staff members often asked, "Are you Theresa's sister?" They guided me to OU's Native community.

I joined Gamma Delta Pi, Incorporated (GDP) and changed my major from premed to Native American Studies (NAS). My GDP sisters, peers, and Native faculty and staff on campus became family. My partner, Zach, and roommate, Millie, were the hands that continually pushed me uphill when I slid backward. Professors Heather Shotton, Barbara Hobson, and Jerry Bread in NAS took me in as their own. One of my most fond memories in NAS came when I lost focus and my GPA began to dip. Professor Hobson pulled me into her office and asked about my plans after graduation. When I told her I wanted to go to graduate school, she quickly replied, "Not with these grades. You need As from here on out, so get it together." My jaw was in my lap at the time, but without this tough love, I may not have qualified for graduate school.

Professors Shotton and Bread sparked my interest in higher education. Both are alumni of OU's Adult and Higher Education Program, and even though I was set on social work, they always pushed me to consider education. Professor Shotton introduced me to the National Indian Education Association (NIEA) and other opportunities in higher education. Due to their persistence, I chose to apply to OU's Adult and Higher Education program. Although I graduated with a bachelor's degree in NAS, they both actively mentored me through my master's program and remain support-ive in my doctoral program as well as in my professional and personal life. Aside from my mentors, my partner, colleagues, family, friends, and students provide unconditional support and remind me every single day why I have chosen this career and educational path.

Above all else, my people inspire me. One of the greatest challenges I faced in college, especially graduate school, was reconciling my need to maintain ties to my people with my passion for higher education. Grow-ing up, I knew I would go to college, but I always had a sense that going to college meant that you had to choose between your education and culture. I was fearful that I would go to college and lose my Cheyenne and Arapaho identity. This perception is all too common in many Native communities, and many students feel they must separate themselves from their culture to find success. Debunking this myth directly drives my work in higher educa-tion, and I want students to know that I have made it this far because of my people and the ways they taught me. You can be Native and successful without sacrificing your ties to your community. Through the support of my family, friends, and community, I know now I do not have to choose. My persistence comes from my people's prayers, and I thrive in higher education because I am Cheyenne and Arapaho. Néá'eše to all those who helped me come to this realization.

MY STORY

Making the Most of College Access Programs

Natalie Rose Youngbull (Southern Cheyenne and Arapaho,
Ft. Peck Sioux and Assiniboine)

I graduated from a tiny high school. My graduating class was only 18 individuals. I did not have access to Advanced Placement (AP) courses, nor did I have access to advanced hard science and math courses, such as physics and calculus. But, I was able to take dual enrollment courses during my senior year, earning 12 credits from my hometown community college. My pursuit of higher education began through participation in the Colorado University Upward Bound (CUUB) program. I was fortunate that my principal and a few teachers were invested in my educational endeavors, encouraging me to apply for the CUUB program as a high school sophomore. CUUB provided access to difficult coursework, including physics and calculus courses, which I thoroughly enjoyed, and it also taught me the ins and outs of the college application process. I remember this being important because my own high school counselor did not provide any guidance on this process. This college prep program equipped me with the knowledge that I needed to be prepared to matriculate and be successful in college.

CUUB was not a typical Upward Bound program. CUUB served Native American students from target high schools from states such as Washington, Oregon, South Dakota, Wyoming, Arizona, New Mexico, Oklahoma, and Colorado. Each summer, up to 140 Native high school students invaded the Colorado University campus in Boulder for the rigorous 6-week residential summer institute. It was there that I gained tangible knowledge about the realm of higher education and experienced living on a major college campus. Through the program, I had the opportunity to read Native American literature and be taught by Native instructors. In all my years in school, my CUUB literature course was the first time I read a book written by a

Native author. The Native instructors were instrumental to us as students because they served as reflections of ourselves, telling us that we belonged in institutions of higher education and that we could be successful.

I remember the first few days of the summer institute were filled with team-building activities, assessment tests, and presentations regarding college knowledge and preparation. The most impactful presentation that has remained with me throughout the years was one on financial aid, which discussed the differences among loans, grants, and scholarships. That was when I realized how much it cost to attend college. I remember telling myself that it did not matter where I went to college, as long as I could get it paid for. During this presentation, I first learned about the Gates Millennium Scholars (GMS) program. My understanding of the GMS was that if I received this scholarship, then I could attend the university of my choice and have it paid for. That's all I needed to know. I was determined to get the Gates Scholarship. I did not know then that the GMS would have such an impact on my life, but to this day I am grateful that CUUB provided the opportunity to learn about such an amazing scholarship. My time spent attending the CUUB summer institutes was very fulfilling. I was challenged beyond what my high school could offer, and I realized the sense of responsibility it took to be successful in college.

In my senior year, I had the opportunity to attend another college prep program. The director of my tribal department of education encouraged me to attend the Tribal Resources in Business, Engineering, and Science (TRIBES) program the summer before entering college. My older brother attended TRIBES a few summers before and spoke highly of his experience, so I decided to take part in it. A 6-week summer residential program at the University of New Mexico, TRIBES served 30 Native American students from across the country. I earned 9 college credits by completing three courses that focused on how to address current issues of tribal governments. The focus on Native nation building made the TRIBES program unique.

Drawing from my personal experience and the knowledge and understanding gained from my educational background, I will take a closer look at how college prep programs create access to higher education for Native American students. First, I discuss the current educational participation gap. Second, I examine the ways that certain college preparation programs create access for Native American students. Third, I discuss the impact of the GMS in Indian Country. I conclude with implications for future research and reflect on the significant role that college prep programs provide to Native American students.

Educational Gap for Access and Attainment

Although enrollment trends for Native American students have steadily increased throughout the last few decades, an educational participation gap remains (Ross et al., 2012). Native American, African American, Hispanic, and low-income students remain underrepresented at institutions of higher education in relation to the overall college-age population (Nettles, Perna, & Freeman, 1999; Ross et al., 2012; Swail & Perna, 2002). Similarly, Ruppert (2003) identified age, race, ethnicity, and socioeconomic status as variables that influence the educational participation gap. Ruppert (2003) also affirmed that, "despite some gains in postsecondary participation and attainment, wide disparities by race and ethnicity persist, and the higher a family's income, the more likely it is to send a high school graduate to college" (p. 3). What is keeping more Native American students from being college bound?

Many researchers support the argument that two forms of capital, social and cultural, play a major role in a student's decision to attend college. Cultural capital is the knowledge and information possessed predominantly by middle- and upper-class families that is shared through generations and is most useful when it is transferred into economic capital (McDonough, 1997). McDonough (1997) acknowledges that all classes have their own cultural capital, but the type of capital held by the middle- and upper-class individuals has the most educational and economic value. Social capital is recognized as the relationships and networks that create access to institutions and support (Stanton-Salazar, 1997). Because many Native American students come from families that do not possess these highly valued forms of capital, they are at a major disadvantage in terms of access to and attainment in institutions of higher education.

In addition to the absence of middle- and upper-class social and cultural capital among many Native American families, the schools that Native American students attend are also not college preparation focused. More than 90% of Native children attend public schools, more likely in rural settings, but increasingly in urban areas (DeVoe, Darling-Churchill & Snyder, 2008). Alarmingly, overall high school completion rates for Native Americans continue to lag behind the national rate. Recent data revealed that high school dropout rates for Native Americans between the ages of 16 and 24 were among the highest of all ethnic minority groups (Ross et al., 2012). Further, high school graduation rates for Native American students were the lowest of all racial/ethnic groups and, at the time of Faircloth and Tippeconnic's (2010) report, had declined in many states. Additionally, Native American students were likely to be tracked into less rigorous coursework throughout high school. In 2000, Native American high school graduates were the least likely to have completed a core academic track compared with their peers from other racial/ethnic groups (U.S. Department of Education, 2005). Many are underprepared to take the SAT and/or ACT, and may not possess even basic knowledge about these assessment tests. Research reveals that Native American students score below the national average on the SAT (U.S. Department of Education, 2005). Additionally, national studies indicate that Native students are "the least likely to complete core course necessary for college eligibility and preparation" (Brayboy, Fann, Castagno, & Solyom, 2012, p. 35). Overall and over time, Native American students remain underprepared for matriculation into college and typically maintain low enrollment rates within institutions of higher education (Jackson, Smith, & Hill, 2003; Ross et al., 2012; Snyder, Tan, & Hoffman, 2006).

Had I not been involved in college access programs, I, too, would not have met the criteria. In my small high school, the college application and choice process was unknown, and I lacked the knowledge and understanding of financial aid, which is critical for most Native American students to attend college. I would have been unaware of services offered through colleges and universities to help retention efforts and increase graduation rates for Native students. Key aspects of CUUB and TRIBES were introduced and helped me understand college access and retention. These programs provided me the social and cultural capital I was missing and needed to enter and be successful in higher education.

Ways the Programs Create Access

The CUUB and TRIBES programs offered several key aspects to promote access to higher education: residential experience, social component, cultural component, educational opportunities, and funding and financial aid. Each aspect will be discussed in further detail in this section.

Residential Experience

The locations of these programs are instrumental to the development of a Native student's sense of belonging on campus. Located on large predominantly non-Native colleges and universities (NNCUs), the CUUB and TRIBES program participants live in the residential halls with a randomly assigned roommate from the program. The opportunity for Native college students to room with another Native student on campus is typically not an option unless a specific wing or residence hall is reserved for Native American students. The residential experience in CUUB and TRIBES provides students the opportunity to acquire a general understanding of the expectations involved in sharing a living space and how to be a good roommate.

Program participants also receive a student identification card, eat their meals in the dining halls, and have access to the recreation/wellness center, library, and student union just like any other student attending the university. Course schedules for the summer institute are rigorous and based on anticipated coursework for the upcoming year. Similar to actual college schedules, program participants attend courses throughout the day with breaks in between. Evening routines include dinner, free time, and study hall before lights out. The majority of students who attend these programs come from schools located on reservations or rural tribal communities where access to a large NNCU is limited. Spending summer on the campus allows students to gain a level of comfort in that setting as they learn to navigate their way around campus. It also provides them with concrete expectations of college life as they go about a daily structured schedule of coursework, meals in the dining hall, studying, and spending time with friends all while residing in the residence halls.

Social Component

On any campus, incoming Native students usually have to take it upon themselves to seek out the Native presence on campus, whether it is through a cultural center/office, student organization(s), or staff/faculty member. Finding this type of connection can offer a level of comfort to Native students transitioning to the college environment. Embedded within the residential experience, program participants have the opportunity to enjoy the social aspects of campus, such as hanging out at the student union between classes, going to the recreation/wellness center, and eating meals in the dining halls with their friends. In the TRIBES program, our small group of 30 Native American incoming freshmen created a strong bond throughout the summer. Each of us was going to be branching out to different colleges and universities the following fall, but throughout the summer, we had conversations envisioning what it would be like if we all decided to attend the same college and how easy it would be for us to already belong to a Native community on campus. This social component is crucial for Native American students to develop a sense of belonging on campus.

Cultural Component

In addition to the firsthand experience of living on campus, CUUB and TRIBES also offer a cultural component to the students. Because these programs serve Native American students, the staff made it a priority to expose the students to positive role models within Indian Country. The residential advisers, living in the residential halls with the students, were all current Native college students from across the United States. Several instructors were Native and taught courses focused on Native perspectives, such as American Indian Literature. As a student in CUUB, I met Sherman Alexie (1996), from the Spokane and Coeur d'Alene tribes, author of *The Lone Ranger and Tonto Fistfight in Heaven.* Our entire program read the book before his visit. In addition to his presentation to the program, he spent time informally visiting students during our free time. It was important for us, as Native students, to see and interact with individuals who we saw as images of ourselves, especially in the realm of higher education, where Native faculty and staff make up less than 1% of all higher education personnel (Snyder & Dillow, 2015). CUUB and TRIBES made it a priority to include Native staff, instructors, and invited speakers/guests throughout the program. The inclusion of Native professionals was a key cultural component in both programs, allowing also for the inclusion of Native culture, curriculum, and role modeling.

Educational Opportunities

Within the realm of educational opportunities provided by CUUB and TRIBES, students had access to assessment tests, ACT/SAT prep, college fairs, preparation for the college application process, and the earning of college credits. Assessment tests were administered at the beginning of the CUUB summer institute to determine each student's course schedule, including English, math, and science. The rigorous course schedule was a combination of building on the previous academic year's courses and preparing for the next year's coursework. The assessment tests provided motivation for students to test as high as they could to be placed in more rigorous courses during the summer institute. I recall challenging ourselves and each other to do well on the assessment tests to get into the most difficult courses. Additionally, we all took an ACT prep test at the beginning of the summer institute, and the results were included in our CUUB report card that we received at the end of the summer institute.

The CUUB program hosted an annual two-day college fair during the summer institute. Numerous college and university staff, from local and regional institutions to the Ivy Leagues, participated by leading small- and large-group presentations and staffing booths in order to interact with students, provide information, and answer questions. College recruiters walked us through the application process, provided tips, and introduced their campus culture and support networks in small break-out sessions. This design allowed us to have as much one-on-one time as we needed with the college recruiters and scholarship representatives.

As current college students, the resident advisers (RAs) offered a panel focused on their personal experiences at their respective colleges/universities. Each panelist answered questions from students and spoke honestly about his or her struggles and achievements. This panel was popular because it provided an opportunity to hear directly from Native college students about their successes and struggles in higher education. Because the RAs were not much older, their experiences resonated with us.

In the TRIBES program, students earned nine credits, tuition free, through the University of New Mexico. The courses—Algebra I, American Indian Literature, and Introduction to Native American Studies (NAS)—allowed us to incorporate current tribal government topics/issues into our learning. For example, in the NAS course, we worked in small groups to research and share specific aspects of contemporary tribal governments. At the end of the summer, we gave formal presentations addressing issues confronting each of the tribes being studied, and we offered recommendations to deal with these issues in front of invited tribal leaders.

Funding and Financial Aid

Understanding the financial aid system is as important for success in higher education as a student's level of preparedness. CUUB and TRIBES arranged presentations to discuss this important topic with students. During the CUUB college fair, representatives from the Gates Millennium Scholars Program, American Indian Graduate Center (AIGC), and the American Indian College Fund presented scholarship opportunities to the students. The TRIBES program hosted a session with a university financial aid adviser who presented information on financial aid packages and how to understand the cost of attendance. As a result of these presentations, students were made aware of avenues for funding within institutions of higher education, nonprofit organizations, foundations, and tribal education departments. This knowledge helped to ease the sticker shock many of us felt when presented with the actual cost associated with college enrollment.

Impact of the GMS Program

Recognizing that many low-income, first-generation underrepresented students are in need of financial assistance to pursue higher education, the Bill & Melinda Gates Foundation created GMS. GMS, or the Gates, is a merit-based scholarship for high-achieving, low-income minority students (Tippeconnic & Faircloth, 2008). One thousand scholarships are awarded annually to high-achieving students with significant financial need from four backgrounds: American Indian/Alaska Native, African American, Asian American/Pacific Islander, and Hispanic American. The AIGC, a private nonprofit entity focused on providing funding to American Indian/Alaska Native college undergraduate and graduate students, oversees the Native American cohort of GMS.

Since GMS's inception in 1999, the program has funded 150 Native American students annually and more than 17,000 from across the nation (The Gates Millennium Scholars, n.d.). These students attend public and private universities, including tribal colleges and universities. Students are funded in the major of their choice for their bachelor's degree and are eligible for funding through graduate school if they continue on in one of seven specific fields of study (Tippeconnic & Faircloth, 2008).[1] GMS goes beyond providing scholarship funding; it also offers social and developmental support services through the Academic Empowerment (ACE) program, which provides academic assistance and peer mentoring between incoming freshmen and senior scholars. Access to national networks and professional development opportunities is another focus of ACE. By establishing an unprecedented funding opportunity for students to attend the college of their choice and pursue any major, the GMS established a national standard for creating financial access for Native American students nationwide.

My dissertation research examines the experiences of American Indian Gates Millennium Scholars (AIGMS) who did not persist to graduation. The story driving this research topic is about a young man from one of my tribal communities. He graduated valedictorian of his high school, was awarded the Gates scholarship, and decided to attend a small, regional four-year institution close to home. I remember thinking that he made a good decision because he comes from a tight-knit community. Within his first year, he left the university and returned home. When I heard this news, it plagued me. His story caused me to ponder the factors that contributed to his exit from the university when he had such a great opportunity through the Gates scholarship.

Overall, Gates Millennium Scholars boast significant retention and graduation rates. The first-year retention rate is 97.9%, and the second-year rate only slightly dips to 96%. The 5-year graduation rate is 82.8%, whereas the 6-year graduation rate jumps to 87.8% (The Gates Millennium Scholars, n.d.). I was unable to locate the retention and graduation rates specifically for AIGMS but was once told by a former GMS employee that the AIGMS cohort has the lowest graduation rate of all 4 cohorts. Currently, literature on the impact of the Gates scholarship on student access and achievement is scant. Tippeconnic and Faircloth's (2008) study analyzing the first 2 years of AIGMS, and comparing them to nonrecipient Native college students, is the only literature focused on this particular group. In this study, AIGMS acknowledged that, beyond substantial financial assistance, GMS encouraged them to persevere in their coursework, magnified their abilities, boosted their self-confidence, and provided them an opportunity to become leaders in their tribal communities (Tippeconnic & Faircloth, 2008). Recognizing the positive impact the GMS has on Native students, my research aims to highlight the influences of home and the campus climate on those AIGMS who did not persist to graduation.

Implications for Future Research

In this chapter, I featured two long-standing college-prep programs geared specifically to serve and prepare college-bound Native American students. CUUB has been in existence for more than 30 years and is part of the federally funded TRIO programs, but it is one of the only Upward Bound programs nationwide that specifically serves Native American high school students. The TRIBES program, which is no longer in existence, introduced sovereign nation building and provided a jump start to college for incoming freshmen from predominantly reservation and tribal communities. Beyond these programs, numerous other programs exist across the nation to encourage college-going among Native students. Research needs to be conducted on these programs to gain a greater understanding of their structure, philosophy, and overall impact on participants' access and success in higher education.

Research comparing the college-going rates of Native American students who attended college-prep programs and those who did not attend is essential to producing a greater understanding of the significance of these types of programs. Specifically, exploring the impact of college-prep programs on Native students' transition and success in college would offer insight into the program characteristics that promote access and attainment. Researchers should never underestimate the power of Native students' stories of struggle and success. Through these stories, students elaborate on the knowledge and experiences that helped them realize their potential to persevere.

As the GMS is nearing its twentieth anniversary,[2] data should be analyzed on its overall impact on the AIGMS cohort. Tippeconnic and Faircloth (2008) recommend comparing Gates Millennium Scholars with nonrecipient first-generation college students' experiences with persistence to graduation, financial aid, causes of deferment, and occupation status. For greater insight into factors affecting Native American student persistence, more research is necessary to understand the impact of services offered through GMS to assist recipients through their educational endeavors, such as the ACE program. In addition, studies on the impact of financial aid for AIGMS need to be explored, with particular attention to decisions to defer or depart from college. Specifically, Tippeconnic and Faircloth (2008) advocate for research to highlight the impact of GMS "on developing leadership skills and improving the quality of life for Native people" (p. 134). Likewise, there is a need for research on GMS's role in AIGMS identity development and networking/professional growth in college. Numerous research opportunities on this particular population of students could improve the knowledge and understanding of Native American student access and attainment in higher education.

Conclusion

My high school was ill equipped to prepare me for college. Growing up, I loved school and learning and was encouraged by my family and community to pursue higher education. However, I never experienced an atmosphere where I was academically challenged, either by my instructors or my peers. I am indebted to these college-prep programs. They provided me with the necessary knowledge, skills, and experience to positively influence my educational journey during my most vulnerable time. These programs provided the opportunity for me to feel comfortable on a college campus by learning how to navigate it, in addition to introducing the rigor and expectations of college courses. The foundation for my academic success is the knowledge and experience I gained through the CUUB and TRIBES programs. The best gift these programs gave me was to be among highly motivated Native students who were not afraid to push each other to excel, to achieve. My successes in higher education would not have been realized without these college-prep programs.

At the end of both programs, I remember experiencing a rush of emotions. Due to the rigorous nature of these programs, I was sleep deprived trying to ace final exams and perfect final projects and presentations. I was eager to see my family, show them around campus, and introduce them to my friends in the program. I had a mix of excitement and sorrow about the end of the program because it meant that I had successfully completed a challenging load of courses, but now it was time to say goodbye to everyone. I remember we bought journals and passed them around for everyone to sign in those last few days of the program. In those journals, we shared favorite memories of the summer, well wishes for the upcoming school year, how much we were going miss each other, and our contact information to keep in touch. In moments of struggle, I return to those journal entries, and I'm reminded of how blessed I am to have that shared experience with so many wonderful Native youth aspiring for success. Embedded in all this, I realized the programs enabled me to be comfortable preparing to move on to higher education. I did not fear the process and all the steps involved. I was confident navigating my way around campus because I learned how to advocate for myself and where to go for assistance. Ultimately, participating in these college-prep programs allowed me to become savvy with college knowledge.

The decision to continue on to graduate school was easy because I had guaranteed funding through GMS. Who would turn that opportunity down? Knowing that no one in my family ever received that type of funding, I knew I had to make the most of this opportunity. This path was laid out for me, and I feel like I am coming full circle with my dissertation research focused on the AIGMSs' experiences in college and the reasons they did not persist to graduation. I want to build my research agenda around this population. It is a way for me to contribute meaningful work and give back to an organization that has been influential in my educational journey.

Notes

1. The seven fields eligible for graduate-level funding are computer science, education, engineering, library science, mathematics, public health, or science.

2. At the time of publication, the Gates Millennium Scholars Program was not accepting new applications but continued to fund all current scholars.

References

Brayboy, B. M. J., Fann, A. J., Castagno, A. E., & Solyom, J. A. (2012). Postsecondary education for American Indian and Alaska Natives: Higher education for nation building and self-determination. *ASHE Higher Education Report, 37*(5), 1–154.

DeVoe, J. F., Darling-Churchill, K. E., & Snyder, T. (2008). *Status and trends in the education of American Indian and Alaska Natives: 2008* (NCES 2008-084). Washington DC: National Education for Educational Statistics, Institute of Education Sciences, U.S. Department of Education.

Faircloth, S. C., & Tippeconnic III, J. W. (2010). *The dropout/graduation rate crisis among American Indian and Alaska Native students: Failure to respond places the future of Native peoples at risk.* Los Angeles, CA: The Civil Rights Project/Proyecto Derechos Civiles at UCLA.

Jackson, A. P., Smith, S. A., & Hill, C. L. (2003). Academic persistence among Native American college students. *Journal of College Student Development, 44*(4), 548–565.

McDonough, P. M. (1997). *Choosing colleges: How social class and schools structure opportunity.* Albany, NY: State University of New York Press.

Nettles, M. T., Perna, L. W., & Freeman, K. E. (1999). *Two decades of progress: African Americans moving forward in higher education.* Fairfax, VA: Frederick D. Patterson Research Institute.

Ross, T., Kena, G., Rathbun, A., KewalRamani, A., Zhang, J., Kristapovich, P., & Manning, E. (2012). *Higher education: Gaps in access and persistence study (NCES 2012-046).* Washington DC: U.S. Government Printing Office.

Ruppert, S. S. (2003, October). *Closing the college participation gap: A national summary.* Denver, CO: Education Commission of the States.

Snyder, T. D., & Dillow, S. A. (2015). *Digest of Education Statistics 2013* (NCES 2015-011). Washington DC: National Center for Education Statistics, Institute of Education Sciences, U.S. Department of Education.

Snyder, T. D., Tan, A. G., & Hoffman, C. M. (2006). *Digest of education statistics 2005 (NCES 2006-030).* Washington DC: U.S. Government Printing Office.

Stanton-Salazar, R. D. (1997). A social capital framework for understanding the socialization of racial minority children and youth. *Harvard Educational Review, 67,* 1–33.

Swail, W. S., & Perna, L. W. (2002). Pre-college outreach programs: A national perspective. In W. G. Tierney & L. S. Hagedorn (Eds.), *Increasing access to college: Extending possibilities for all students* (pp. 15–34). Albany, NY: State University of New York Press.

The Gates Millennium Scholars. (n.d.). *About us.* Retrieved from http://www.gmsp .org/gates-millennium-scholars-program/

Tippeconnic III, J. W., & Faircloth, S. C. (2008). Socioeconomic and cultural characteristics of high-achieving and low-income American Indian and Alaska Native college students: The first two years of the Gates Millennium Scholars Program (Vol. 23). In W. T. Trent & E. P. St. John (Eds.), *Readings on equal education: Resources, assets, and strengths among successful diverse students: Understanding the contributions of the Gates Millennium Scholars Program* (pp. 107–141). New York, NY: AMS Press, Inc.

U.S. Department of Education. (2005). *Status and trends in the education of American Indians and Alaska Natives (NCES 2005-108).* Washington DC: U.S. Government Printing Office.

2

TOUGH CONVERSATIONS AND "GIVING BACK"

Native Freshman Perspectives on the College Application Process

Adrienne Keene (Cherokee)

Sitting with a young, charismatic Native first-year college student, I ask him about applying to college. We talk back and forth about his decision process: the stress, the heartache, the difficult conversations with his parents, and the challenges he faced despite a supportive family, a strong college counselor at his high school, and help from community-based college access organizations.

As a Native student, this young man's voice and perspective on his college process is important. In this chapter, I examine the perspectives of two Native students on their college application and decision processes to raise questions about the ways to best serve such a diverse population and address the particular needs of Native students in this transitional time in their lives. I conclude with a discussion of implications for educators, families, and communities. The data for this discussion come from a larger portraiture (Lawrence-Lightfoot & Hoffman Davis, 1997) study that followed four students through their freshman year in college in the 2012–2013 school year (Keene, 2014). The students are all alumni of a precollege access program for Native students called College Horizons (CH).

Founded in 1999, CH is an annual week-long summer program serving American Indian, Alaska Native, and Native Hawaiian students and is hosted on one to two college campuses around the country. By the end of a nonstop week, students from CH emerge with a completed common application, a personalized list of 10 schools that match their needs and abilities, and a polished personal essay draft, and they are armed with vocabulary and knowledge about financial aid, letters of recommendation, and the specific triumphs and challenges of being not just a student in college, but a *Native* student in college. The program was founded by Whitney Laughlin, a non-Native college counselor with a long history of working with students from underresourced backgrounds, and is now under the leadership of Carmen Lopez (Navajo).

The motto of the program, "College Pride, Native Pride," embodies the goals of the program—instilling knowledge and pride in college-going while cultivating and supporting pride in Native heritage. As much of the research and statistics in the introduction of this book demonstrate, when placed in contrast to non-Natives, Native students fall below their peers in high school graduation, college-going, and college graduation rates (DeVoe, Darling-Churchill, & Snyder, 2008). In this context and educational landscape, CH presents the other side of the story, boasting that 99% of their program alumni enroll directly in college, 95% in 4-year institutions, and 85% graduate from college in 5 years (College Horizons, n.d.)—all accomplished with a full-time staff of only 3 and a budget much smaller than many comparable programs.

CH is structured with a nearly two-to-one student-to-faculty ratio, with the program faculty consisting of college admission officers from various "partner schools" around the country, ranging from small liberal arts schools to highly selective Ivy League institutions and large state schools. In addition to the admissions officers, guidance and college counselors from elite private high schools volunteer to provide one-on-one college counseling that Native students may not receive in their home environments. Finally, the remainder of the faculty is made up of Native community members and volunteer counselors from Native schools and community organizations. Faculty members are assigned specific roles in the group, and each works closely with individual students throughout the program.

Each program serves approximately 100 rising high school juniors and seniors, and the curriculum is split between "large-group" sessions, where faculty present overviews of concepts such as financial aid and personal qualities in the admission process, and "small-group" time, where students work closely with the faculty members in groups of 10 to 12 to accomplish their goals for the week and solidify and put into practice the large-group session information. These small groups form tight bonds throughout the week, and it is not uncommon for faculty and students to stay in touch throughout the application process and beyond.

Native identities and discussions are wrapped in throughout the week, with a local elder's prayer opening and closing the program; a "traditional night," where students are invited to share talents and cultural knowledge from their home communities; and explicit discussions of education as a tool of nation building, colonialism, representations, and more.

As a Cherokee woman, I have been involved with CH as a student, faculty member, and researcher. The students in this chapter were part of my small group, where I served as their essay specialist, helping them to refine and polish their college personal statements. I subsequently followed up with them after they enrolled in college, interviewing them approximately once a month and visiting them on their college campuses and at home. In this chapter, I examine the "college application process": the processes surrounding the selection of a list of undergraduate colleges to which to apply; the filling out and submitting of the college applications, scholarship applications, and financial aid forms; and the decision process of where to matriculate.

An aspect of the college application process I encounter through the students' stories is the idea of "giving back" through higher education. This thread runs through much of the literature on Native students in college, demonstrating that students often express a strong desire to "give back" to their communities (Brayboy, 2005; Guillory & Wolverton, 2008; Huffman, 2011; Lee, 2009). Guillory and Wolverton (2008) note that "a college education meant more than just a means to obtaining a career and financial independence; for these students, it was an instrument to combat deleterious conditions back home" (p. 75). Jackson, Smith, and Hill (2003) identified a more complicated relationship between students and their home communities, calling it "paradoxical cultural pressure" (p. 558). They point out that many of their study subjects "indicated a desire to return to their reservation to help the people there. Others said that they had to cut their connections to the reservation as a means of maintaining their success" (Jackson et al., 2003, p. 560).

Many of the studies that highlight "giving back" focus on reservation-raised students or "culturally traditional" students (Guillory & Wolverton, 2008; Huffman, 2011; Jackson et al., 2003), who are placed in opposition to "assimilated" students, or those with less strong cultural ties. Huffman (2011) found in a quantitative study of 86 Native college students that a desire to use higher education to serve Native peoples was associated with being female, coming from a reservation, attending high school with a large Native population, and having a "traditional cultural orientation." In contrast, a desire to use higher education as a means of financial gain was associated with being younger and entering college soon after high school and having less of a traditional cultural orientation. Finally, Huffman (2011) found an association between planning to serve Native communities and planning to live/move back to a reservation. "Giving back" has traditionally been seen as a commitment to returning to a reservation environment, but I am curious whether students see their service to Indian Country more broadly or in new or diverse ways and how that relationship may or may not appear earlier in the college application process. In the next section, I provide two student perspectives.

Student Perspectives[1]

Caitlin

Caitlin is a member of a tribe in the eastern part of the United States. She was raised off her reservation in numerous southern states but moved to the reservation in high school after her parents divorced. After a tough transition, she now sees her tribal community as her home and is dedicated to coming back to work for her community as a doctor. She now attends a top-ranked private university, where her major is premed.

When Caitlin first moved to the reservation, her mom thought, in Caitlin's words, "Yeah, [the kids will] go to the tribal school, you know get to know their culture, they'll be good anywhere they go!" The high school on the reservation is a beautiful facility, rivaling any small college campus. The walls are covered in stonework mimicking traditional basketry designs, and the athletic facilities are all top of the line, with a football field of expensive artificial grass. However, the inside of the school doesn't necessarily match the outside. According to Caitlin, the academic rigor of the curriculum is not known to be the best, and college-going is not seen as a focus. Caitlin's non-Native dad said, again in Caitlin's words,

> "My kids will never go to a tribal school . . . not as long as I have a say they're not." So he came to the reservation and checked out the local schools, ultimately deciding on a small public school 15 minutes off the reservation, and said, "This is where they're going to go."

Despite greater access to advanced coursework, at Caitlin's off-reservation high school, the college-going culture was, according to Caitlin, "very laid back." They had one guidance counselor who served their 130-student senior class, but "you had to be determined to go to college and to go out there and take care of yourself, because everyone wasn't going to college." Like many high schools in the South, a big emphasis was placed on athletics, and academics could sometimes take a back seat. Caitlin estimates that about 75 of her classmates went on to some form of college—more than half of the graduating class.

"[For my] roommate [at college], every single person that graduated at her high school went to college, but it wasn't like that at my school. It was, I think . . . I want to say 30% went to community college and 30% went to

4-year college." Caitlin was motivated academically, which was challenging in an environment that stressed athletics. "It's hard to balance when there's such a push for athletics and being in sports. I was real involved in all the other organizations and things and balancing that with class . . . but most people weren't taking AP classes." Caitlin came to appreciate the fact that fewer of her classmates were engaged in the Advanced Placement program because it meant she was able to build up close relationships with her teachers. In many ways, she felt that disconnect between the sports culture and academic culture made it "not *easier*, but nicer." Because it was "the same seven people pretty much taking those classes," the community could become close knit.

Caitlin seems sure of herself as she tells me these stories, as though there never was another option besides finding success in her advanced classes. I'm curious where her motivation came from, both to take the classes as well as work hard to be successful. She answers honestly, "Well, I don't know," and then she continues,

> I just always thought it was important to do the best you can, because your parents raise you—and shouldn't you be the best you can for them and for the community, and the people that helped you? So [then] you can give the community, give back in the best way you can, and help as many people as possible. . . . I mean, isn't that the point of life, to help people and to give back? Other than, you know, your biological reasons. . . .

She laughs. "But, you know, I just feel like for all the people that helped me it's my duty to try my hardest to help them and future generations." I hear the language of nation building in her response, thinking about ideas of "giving back" so you can support those who came before you but also those who will come after you. To me, it's so amazing to hear a young woman talk so passionately about the "point of life" being to help others in her community.

Similar to many of the students I've worked with through the years at CH, Caitlin found her college process to be straightforward once she got back home from the week-long program, and she attributed that ease to her experience at CH:

> [The application process] ran so much smoother! Because of that I had an essay ready. I had a list of colleges that I wanted to go to. Meeting the people through the admissions office, that was amazing—to actually get to go and talk with them and, you know, run in the morning with some of them and form a relationship. That was special. To pick those colleges that I was interested in and already have those ready to go and just start the common application. I already pretty much knew how it worked and just filled in everything. It was much smoother.

Caitlin ended up applying to "Cornell, Brown, Johns Hopkins, Harvard, Yale, Penn State, the University of Mississippi, University of Georgia, Denver University, Wake Forest, Chapel Hill, and Duke." She lists them off easily and quickly—12 schools in all. Of this group, she "didn't get into any of the Ivy Leagues," which, as a former admission officer, surprises me, knowing Caitlin's academic profile. She continues, "I got in obviously to [this one], and then [that one and that one] and [that one, that one, that one] . . ." she trails off, with a laugh, "I can't remember!"

Her decision process for settling on her current university brought together a number of factors, and her CH connections played a role as well. Caitlin had originally thought she'd end up at her parents' alma mater:

> I had always been set on going [there] because that's where my parents went and we'd always go to football games there and that was home. But it was a hard decision. It really was. But [my school] is closer to home than there. . . . Five hours west is mom and then five hours south is dad. . . . So, it's kind of a central good spot.

The distance from home became a primary factor in her decision, but her experience at her university's admitted student weekend solidified the choice for her, and Paul, the admission representative at CH, made sure the weekend was tailored for Caitlin's interests:

> [Paul] who I met at CH—he kept in touch with me and he remembered me and said, "you were interested in this university, right?" I said yes and so he said, "I want to bring you and have you stay for a weekend for [admitted student] days." He set me up to stay with a girl who was from [a town] close to me in the mountains. So, I stayed with her and I got to kind of experience life at [this school] and living here, and there was a whole bunch of different activities to do.

I ask her, "What was it about the campus that made you feel like that was a place that could be your home for the next four years?" I've learned through working with Caitlin that "home" is really important to her, and I wonder how the campus made her feel comfortable enough to see it as her next home. "Well, besides the beautiful gothic architecture," she begins, and I smile, but she has thought much deeper than surface beauty. Caitlin explained,

> It was that people were all very nice but they were respectful and knowledge-able. I just liked the aura it gave off. Everything about it just seemed phe-nomenal. All the opportunities and how they have smaller classrooms. It's

not so overwhelming with huge lectures. Our class, there's only like 1,700 of us and so it's not an overwhelming size. There are so many academic support systems and tutor centers and study groups that I can be involved in. That was really—several things that drove me to [this university].

The response seems like a perfect Caitlin response—both pragmatic and practical, citing the tutoring and "academic support systems," but also the optimistic and intangible, with the kindness of the community and "aura" of the campus factoring in her decision.

John

John is a member of a southwest tribe, raised primarily on his reservation, except for the early years of his life when he lived in another state as his mother finished college. He now lives with his mother, stepfather, and younger brother on the reservation. Both his mother and stepfather have bachelor's degrees and are employed by the tribe, and John's stepfather is also a traditional healer. John is premed and wishes to combine traditional medicine and teachings with Western medicine. He attends a highly competitive BA/MD program at a regional state university.

John and I pull into the parking lot of his former school on the reservation. We park in the dirt and gravel parking lot and make our way down a set of iron steps to the campus below. The school was built in the early 1900s and has had some major additions since then, but the original buildings remain and are still in use today. John attended the school from fourth grade through high school; a large portion of his schooling happened on this small campus. The school is a Catholic school, the oldest buildings are church buildings, stone with stained glass windows and bell towers; as we walk around the perimeter of the school grounds, statues of saints are scattered throughout.

We enter the main school building and approach the main desk. John says, "I can't believe it's been a year since I've been back here!" There were 32 students in John's graduating class, and according to John, the teachers "really pushed" the students to be academically successful. The school boasts a "nearly 95%" graduation rate for its students. One teacher in particular, their English teacher, really pushed college-going and would help students with the application process for schools and scholarships. John thinks about 12 of the students in his graduating class went on to the Armed Forces, whereas the rest, at least "most of them," are in some form of college.

John has taken advantage of numerous opportunities such as CH, summer school at a prep school in New Hampshire, and an internship at the National Institutes of Health in Maryland. These experiences took him off the reservation and gave him new perspectives, but he also experienced ignorance and direct racism from his peers at these programs. At a panel he participated in at his high school, John talked about some of the comments from fellow students he received at the prep school. "They stereotyped me," he said. "One even asked, 'Where's your feather?'" John avoided telling the other students his tribe because "I didn't know how to deal with that type of stereotype."

We walk around the interior of the main building, with John pointing out classrooms and other points of interest. Along the walls are graduation portraits of the seniors dating back to the 1950s and 1960s. We pause every so often to laugh at the hairstyles. But there is also something powerful about seeing those rows and rows of photos, thinking about all of the Native students who have come through this school and graduated. We find John's class photos at the end of the hallway, closest to the principal's office, with the most recent graduating class. We look at the group, and John tells me what each of them is now doing as far as he can remember. I hear a lot of local colleges but am also surprised when he points to two young women and says they are now at a small Catholic college in New Jersey. John says he has heard they get a lot of ignorant questions from classmates. "At least there's two of them," I say, thinking about how important having the support of one another must be so far from home.

John's mom went to a small liberal arts college, and John says that because of this, he always grew up knowing that he would go to college. "She wanted me to go to college *very*, very much, yes," he says. I ask him why he thinks it was important to her for him to go to school. "Well, she always told me to be what I want to be, but also to think about what I want to do with my life. If I want a family, if I want a house, if I want, you know, the luxuries that the world has to offer me, that I'd have to go to school for it. Make a better life than she had. You know, she had me when she was in college."

I ask John whether that motivation—for "making a better life for [himself]"—has still been his primary goal in getting his college degree or whether it has shifted now that he's been in college.

> It actually shifted a lot, yes. Like before, it just seemed like, "I'll go to college, you know, make money, and then we'll be happy." But now I see what physicians actually do, and how hard it is, and how much they help people. And, that's why I want to become a pediatrician and help children. It's—it's less about the money for me now. It's more of about being of service to my people.

Given that he sees his degree as "being of service to [his] people," I ask John a question I've asked all of the students: "Why do you think it's important for Natives to go to college?" I find it interesting and important that he is the first one of the group to question what I mean when I say "Native":

> Well, I think it depends on the person's background. Depends on what you mean by "Native." Are they, do they still . . . do they speak the language? Do they practice their traditions, the cultures? Or are they—they don't really know, are they Catholic or brought up traditional?
>
> Also, you know, if they want to do something with their lives, you know, and, do they want to come back and help the people, they're going to have to get a degree in something. I mean, I always said that if being a doctor doesn't work out, I could be a mechanic. Everybody needs their cars fixed. Everybody needs their tires changed, their oil changed. Stuff like that . . . it mainly depends on the person's cultural background.

I clarify and ask more specifically, "So I guess, more specifically, for Native students from your community, why do you think it's, or do you think it's important for them to go to college?" John is clear that he believes it is first important for them to know where they come from and have a cultural foundation to move forward:

> It's important for them to become accustomed to where they come from. To know the story of their people, know where they come from so they can know where they're going. I mean you know me, I understand [my language]—it's very hard to speak it, but I'm learning through ceremony. I'm learning the [ceremonies] from my stepfather. Actually, he's singing this weekend so I'll be helping him out. Get the sense of foundation—build that foundation of where you come from. So when you go out into the world, so that you know where you're going and you always have something to fall back to.

What I hear in John's answer is that the college degree isn't necessarily the most important goal. Having a grounding and an understanding of culture and place from which they come is the first step. Because without that foundation, they won't know why they need to come back and won't have the right lens with which to view their work in the community.

When John was thinking about where he was going to go to school, he initially was considering going to a small liberal arts school in Wisconsin that has been supportive of CH and Native students in the last few years. But for John, it wasn't just his decision. He "talked to [his] parents and extended family," and they "encouraged [him] to look at this BA/MD program [at the regional state university]." Consequently, he applied to the regional state university and was admitted. When he thinks about Wisconsin, he admits,

"It was pretty farfetched," but he knows that he would have been premed wherever he ended up, but this was just a "more direct route." I ask him whether he was worried about going to school so far from home. "Yeah," he says, without hesitation.

> I did an internship over the summer at the National Institutes of Health. . . . And, seeing everybody, seeing how the city works and everything. . . . I don't think I would have lived there. It's very hard. I just chose a place closer to home and where I can study premed.

I think it's important to look at John's decision process, especially how he brings up his parents and his extended family as the main motivation for his decision to apply to college. For John, the college decision process truly is a much more collective endeavor. This isn't just about him, what he wants to study, and where he wants to go; it involves more than just him as an individual.

Lessons and Implications

In listening to Caitlin and John, several lessons and implications emerge. I present them in a series of questions we, as educators, community members, and supporters, can ask ourselves to better understand and serve Native students in this process.

Who Are the Native Students We Are Serving?

In the literature on Native students in postsecondary education, the most common story is one of a low-income, first-generation, reservation-raised Native student. However, the diversity of Indian Country is different than that narrow scope. Although that experience is valid and important, how do we begin to understand the diversity of experience, perspective, and access to resources of Native students? The students in this chapter challenge some of the dominant "tropes" of Native students with mixed-race perspectives, suburban and reservation perspectives, private school experiences, public school experiences, and highly educated parents. When creating programming or supports for Native students in the application process, which segments of Indigenous students are we targeting? How can we be more inclusive of the multiplicity of Native identities and experiences?

How Are We Serving Students?

It becomes clear from the student stories that there is no "one-size-fits-all" approach to how best assist Native students through the college application process. There is a need for cultural competency and understanding from the advising side because guidance counselors and colleges need to understand the specific challenges and needs of Native students. We must ask ourselves: What are the resources available to Native students on your campus? Are they meeting the cultural, academic, and social needs of your students? Are there varied resources and support to meet the needs of all students?

How Are We Involving Family and Community in the College Application Process?

A thread that winds through these student stories is that of family involvement in the college application process. For non-Native students, "helicopter" parents who are overly involved in the college process are often seen as a detriment, whereas for Native students, connections with family can be seen as extensions of Indigenous ways of knowing that emphasize the collective over the individual. Rather than delaying adulthood, family involvement is a key factor in letting Native students feel comfortable with decisions throughout the process and will ultimately allow them to find success. How can we better see family involvement as positive for Native students? How are high schools and colleges creating avenues to also inform and connect to students' families and tribal communities?

How Are We Supporting and Encouraging Nation Building?

In addition to family as motivation and support, Native students often list "giving back" as a motivator, and this is key for colleges to tap into. How will you make the degree relevant for students and their communities? What kinds of coursework, internships, or other opportunities for community involvement are there for Native students on campus? As these two students show, there is a strong desire to support and make positive change in communities through education, and there is a responsibility for colleges to assist in that process. If we wish to have Native students on our campuses, then we need to make sure their needs, including the ability to give back, are being met.

How Can Native Communities Better Support Native Students?

The current model for many tribal education departments seems to offer support to college-going students solely by offering scholarships but not much else in relation to support or services that students may need. Many programs, such as CH, offer assistance to students navigating the college process, but they require applications, recommendations, and essays to attend. In this space, communities can step up by offering encouragement and assistance in applying to these programs through local in-person support from a tribal education department or virtual online support for students living outside of tribal lands. This structure can continue through the college application process, extending into navigating the complexities of taxes and financial aid forms and enhancing a community's ability to remain abreast of opportunities for families and students, as well as any changes in forms, regulations, and institutional and tribal policies.

Conclusion

Both Caitlin and John have completed their bachelor's degrees, and each of them has been through struggles and triumphs along the way. After studying abroad in Kushan, China, during her undergraduate program, Caitlin is now entering medical school. John has continued to excel in his coursework through determination, including many early mornings, and has entered the medical school portion of his joint BA/MD program. He still heads home to the reservation to assist his stepfather with ceremonies when he can.

In much of the literature on the college application and decision process for Native students, we hear about students without hearing their voices and perspectives. Native students remain incredibly invisible in college, and being able to see them as individuals is an important step in humanizing and demystifying the process. Through these two student voices, we can begin to see the needs of students during this complicated and often contentious time of transition from high school to college. To better serve Native students in the college pipeline, we need to see them as individuals as well as part of communities and families.

Note

1. All student names are pseudonyms.

References

Brayboy, B. M. J. (2005). Transformational resistance and social justice: American Indians in Ivy League universities. *Anthropology and Education Quarterly, 36*(3), 193–211.

College Horizons. (n.d.). *Filling in the college access gap*. Retrieved from http://www.collegehorizons.org/about

DeVoe, J. F., Darling-Churchill, K. E., & Snyder, T. D., (2008). *Status and trends in the education of American Indians and Alaska Natives* (NCES 2008). Washington

DC: National Center for Education Statistics, Institute of Education Sciences, U.S. Department of Education.

Guillory, R. M., & Wolverton, M. (2008). It's about family: Native American student persistence in higher education. *The Journal of Higher Education, 79*(1), 58–87.

Huffman, T. E. (2011). Plans to live on a reservation following college among American Indian students: An examination of transculturation theory. *Journal of Research in Rural Education, 26*(3), 1–13.

Jackson, A., Smith, S., & Hill, C. (2003). Academic persistence among Native American college students. *Journal of College Student Development, 44*(4), 548–565.

Keene, A. J. (2014). "College pride, native pride" and education for Native nation building: Portraits of Native students navigating freshman year. Unpublished dissertation, Harvard University.

Lawrence-Lightfoot, S., & Hoffmann Davis, J. (1997). *The art and science of portraiture.* San Francisco, CA: Jossey Bass.

Lee, T. S. (2009). Building Native nations through Native students' commitment to their communities. *Journal of American Indian Education, 48*(1), 19–36.

MONTY'S STORY

Monty Begaye (Diné)

My name is Monty Begaye. I am an enrolled member of the Diné (Navajo) Nation. I am Kin'yá'ání (Towering House clan), born for Ná'k'ái Diné'e (Mexican People clan), my maternal grandparents are Tah'né'za'ní (Tangled People clan), and my paternal grandparents are Kin'yá'ání (Towering House clan). I grew up in a single-parent household, and I am the first in my family to have attained a college degree. I am from Tuba City, Arizona. Tuba City is a small town located on the western edge of the Navajo reservation. In 2009, I graduated from Tuba City High School (TCHS), and I began my journey at the University of Arizona (UA) that same summer. I participated in the New Start Summer Program, which is a summer bridge program for first-year students who have committed to attend the UA the following fall semester.

I earned my bachelor of science in public management and policy in 2014, followed by a master of arts in American Indian studies (AIS) in 2016, also from UA. I am currently a PhD student studying adult and higher education at the University of Oklahoma (OU). I am proud of where I am. I never thought that I would pursue and accomplish a graduate-level education. Prior to pursuing graduate school, I assumed that a bachelor's degree would be my stopping point, and then I would have returned home and sought out employment in my home community.

My original goal to attend college was to own nice things. Later, my college journey changed to a venture of how I could help create access and opportunities in higher education for students who may come from a similar disadvantaged background as mine. Before I went to college, I did not feel like I was a minority, I did not feel like I was living below the national rate of poverty, and I was uninformed about the social injustices that plague Indigenous communities in this nation, even while being immersed in them. I grew up comfortable with everything I needed regardless of being classified as poor. As I progressed in my education, my worldview expanded. Gaining a consciousness of the social ills that plague Native communities allowed my journey to then focus on how I can be a change agent for Indigenous people.

When I first moved to Norman, Oklahoma, I was invited to attend a Multicultural Student Orientation on the OU campus. The orientation began with a larger assembly inside an auditorium. Following the assembly, students were invited to attend smaller colloquiums that presented information about campus resources that might be more appealing to the demographic(s) they identified with. I attended the Native American Student Services presentation. In this session, a graduate of OU's law school spoke about how his Juris Doctor should have his name, as well as the names of those who have helped him along his journey. This statement reminded me of those who have helped me reach my goals and challenged me to pursue aspirations I had only dreamed about and experiences I would not have imagined living.

Gaining access to graduate school was a challenge. The challenge was a fault of my own because I did not do well academically as an undergraduate. My cumulative GPA at the end of my undergraduate program was well below the requirement to be considered for the AIS graduate program at UA, but I was admitted on a provisional status. Because of my low undergraduate GPA, I was also admitted into OU's adult and higher education program under a provisionary status for my first semester. Although my undergraduate program was unsatisfactory, I have done well in my graduate-level programs.

Gaining admittance into both graduate programs was in large part due to the advocacy of Professor Manley Begay, a former faculty member in the UA's AIS program, and Professor Penny Pasque, my current faculty adviser at OU. I also credit Steven Martin, my esteemed mentor, who is presently the director of the Native American Student Affairs program at the UA. Martin encouraged me to take advantage of the opportunities that have prepared me for the future endeavors I will pursue. Of course this list is by no means conclusive.

I aspire to serve in the role of tribal liaison at a mainstream institution once I have earned a PhD and acquired adequate career experience. Under the guidance of my mentors, I was able to pursue an internship in New York City and be named a Fellow with The College Board. Additionally, my mentors have assisted in helping me to create a strong network of supportive higher education professionals. Through this network, I was able to visit campuses, speak with faculty and doctoral students, and reaffirm my choice to pursue a PhD, as well as my professional aspirations.

It is also important for me to acknowledge my family. On the first day of my last semester as an undergraduate, my grandfather passed away. The relationship that I had with my grandfather was unlike any other. I grew up at my family's sheep camp, where I was referred to by family as my "grandfather's tail" because I often followed him everywhere he went. My grandfather was not Western educated. He was a Navajo medicine man who only spoke Navajo, and he instilled in me the importance of maintaining my identity as a Navajo man. Although my grandfather did not fully understand what a Western education entailed, he knew I was doing something great for my family, my community, and the people. He always told me, before I would return to Tucson from school breaks at home, "Yéego int'í, nizhónígó iniłt'á shí cheii (Persevere, do your best in school, grandson)." My grandfather is who I turn to for help, through prayer, when I encounter challenges. My grandfather is someone I acknowledge at each graduation and milestone I reach. His support is unyielding.

Along this journey of higher education, I have met and created lasting bonds with countless individuals. My mentors became family. My classmates and coworkers became my brothers and sisters. The students whom I have worked with became my younger brothers and sisters. I have experienced things that I might not have without a college education. My travels and experiences have equipped me to better serve the people and have provided me opportunities to see things that I had only dreamed of. My family has graciously sacrificed a tremendous amount of unwavering love and support since before I chose to leave home to pursue higher education. I recognize these people and experiences for why I have been able to accomplish all that I have and will.

3

GETTING STARTED LOCALLY

How Tribal Colleges and Universities Are Opening
Doors to the Undergraduate Experience

David Sanders (Oglala Lakota)
and Matthew Van Alstine Makomenaw
(Grand Traverse Bay Band of Ottawa and Chippewa Indians)

Numerous studies and institutions focus on Native American college student retention; however, students must first be enrolled in your institution before you can retain them. College enrollment for American Indian students, while steady, has remained around 1% of all college students from 2000 to 2012 (U.S. Department of Education, 2013). In 2012, there were 98,000 American Indian undergraduates enrolled in 4-year institutions and 74,200 enrolled in 2-year colleges (U.S. Department of Education, 2013). In 2010, tribal colleges and universities (TCUs) served 19,070 students from more than 250 tribal nations (American Indian Higher Education Consortium, 2012). TCUs currently serve approximately 8% of all Native American undergraduates, making them key institutions in helping students access higher education and reach their academic, personal, and professional goals.

College access for the purposes of this chapter is not confined to the ability to be accepted into a university but also having the financial and social resources to attend and succeed in college. For many Native American students, access barriers to college include low high school completion rates, lack of academic preparation, low scores on college entrance exams, and lack of access to those exams (Brayboy, Fann, Castagno, & Solyom, 2012). The cost of higher education is also a detriment to enrollment for underserved populations, including Native Americans (National Center for Public Policy and Higher Education, 2011). As college access becomes more challenging and difficult for all students, TCUs will continue to be significant factors in bridging the college attainment gap for Native students.

In this chapter, we explore how TCUs help students overcome college access barriers. We begin by examining the history and profile of TCUs and why they are vital pathways for Native American students to four-year degrees. We then review how TCUs serve as a pathway to higher education. Finally, we discuss and make recommendations on how TCUs can continue to be efficient and effective institutions in helping Native students access their goals and dreams.

TCU History and Profile

TCUs began in the late 1960s as a way to enhance self-determination and counter the negative experience many Native Americans had in non-Native colleges and universities (NNCUs) (Reyhner & Eder, 2004). TCUs have become culturally responsive and safe institutions for many students who live on or near a reservation (Benham & Stein, 2003; Warner & Gipp, 2009). Furthermore, TCUs focus on developing culturally relevant programs to meet the needs of the Native Americans and the communities they serve (Martin, 2005). Early leaders of the TCU movement hoped to cultivate leaders who were focused on social justice (Ambler, 2005). By design, TCUs were created to empower Native communities' nation-building capacity through access to higher education.

Every tribal college offers associate's degrees, 13 offer bachelor's degrees, and 2 offer master's degrees (AIHEC, 2012). TCUs vary in size of student enrollment, number of degrees offered, and infrastructure. TCUs are uniquely positioned to serve the educational needs of Native American communities. The American Indian Higher Education Consortium (AIHEC) represents the public policy and research interest of 37 TCUs.

TCUs serve a variety of students from different age groups, genders, ethnicities, those with children, and those caring for other family members. A majority of students at TCUs are Native women (AIHEC, 2006), and most students are under the age of 24, with 33% between the ages of 25 and 49, and 4% are over the age of 50 (AIHEC, 2012). TCU students are more likely than other students nationally to have dependents (American Indian College Fund, 2012). Whereas a majority of TCU students are Native American, roughly 16% are not (AIHEC, 2012).

TCUs as College Access Points

In this section, we discuss why TCUs are the institution of choice for many Native students. As previously stated, college access is more than being accepted into college; it involves having the capacity to attend from financial and social perspectives. We examine the role that location, affordability, the percentages of Native American faculty, staff, and students at TCUs, and culture have on access for Native students.

Location

For Native American and Indigenous people all over the world, land and place is sacred and a teacher (Meyer, 2003). The history and process of placing Native Americans on reservations is well documented and an often painful memory. Nonetheless, reservations today mean physical survival, cultural survival, sovereignty, community, and home. Reservations matter to those who grew up on or near them, and the idea of leaving the reservation can be a difficult proposition. The ability to access higher education on reservations means that students can stay close and connected to the past, present, and future of their tribal nations.

A majority of the 37 TCUs are located on reservations and operated by a tribal nation. Haskell Indian Nations University (Haskell) and Southwestern Indian Polytechnic Institute (SIPI) are affiliated with the Bureau of Indian Affairs and draw students from many Tribal nations across the United States. SIPI is represented by more than 100 tribal nations. In addition, the Institute of American Indian Arts (IAIA) is a congressionally chartered college, and its student body is represented by 112 tribal nations. In general, students who attend Haskell, SIPI, and IAIA will have to leave their reservations or homes to attend these TCUs. .

For TCUs located on reservations, the student population is drawn from the local community, meaning that Native students on many reservations have access to higher education without having to leave home. Roughly 22% of people whom self-identify as Native American live on or near reservations (U.S. Census Bureau, 2012). Whereas 78% live off reservation in urban areas (U.S. Census Bureau, 2012), TCUs provide access to education for isolated and high-proportion Native communities.

A majority of TCU students are in close proximity to their family. A contributing factor in collegiate success for Native students is receiving support from family (Guillory & Wolverton, 2008; Jackson, Smith, & Hill, 2003; Makomenaw, 2014). The role of family is a critical aspect of student success, persistence, and retention for TCU students (Ortiz & Heavy Runner, 2003). The location of a higher education institution matters to many Native students, but especially those who live on or near a reservation. TCUs provide students on reservations an opportunity to access education while staying connected to land, nation, and family.

Affordability

The cost of attending college is an access barrier for many Native students. Unemployment and the likelihood to be living in poverty are much higher for Native Americans (Freeman & Fox, 2005). The family income for many TCU students falls below the poverty line (American Indian College Fund, 2008). When making a college choice decision, the cost of education plays a major role for many Native students, making the financial affordability of TCUs the college of choice.

Moreover, family median income is increasing at a slower rate than college tuition increases (National Center for Public Policy & Higher Education, 2011). Rising college tuition cost is making it more difficult for those in financial need to access higher education. The average tuition cost for a full-time TCU student is roughly $2,200 (Institute for Higher Education Policy, 2006). In contrast, in 2007, the average tuition amount for a full-time student at a public 4-year college was $6,185 (College Board, 2007).

In addition to college tuition, the cost of attending college includes room and board; books; and, for many institutions, other miscellaneous fees. TCU students tend to have one or more dependents, which often means the added expense of child care. Attending a TCU allows students to pay less on tuition and fees, live in their current residence, and have access to family members for child-care support.

More than 80% of TCU students rely on financial aid to pay for college (Institute for Higher Education Policy, 2006). The amount of financial aid per person for Native students tends to be less than the national average (Tierney, Sallee, & Venegas, 2007). For many Native students, their tribal nation offers financial assistance for college. Moreover, for students who attend TCUs, they have the opportunity to receive scholarships from the American Indian College Fund (AICF). Although TCUs are a more affordable college option, TCU students rely on multiple forms of assistance to attend college (American Indian College Fund, 2012). Overall, lower tuition, family and community support, and access to multiple sources of funding make TCUs the college of choice.

Native American Faculty, Staff, and Students

TCUs provide Native students with the opportunity to attend a college with a higher percentage of Native American students and faculty. TCUs are required for funding purposes to have a student enrollment of at least 51% who identify as Native American. Of the 19,070 students TCUs serve, roughly 83% are Native American (American Indian Higher Education Consortium, 2012). In contrast, at NNCUs, Native American students will generally represent 1% or less of the student population.

Having access to and interaction with other Native Americans on campus is a key factor in college success and social competence for Native students (Pavel & Inglebret, 2007). TCU students are more comfortable having other Native students on campus (Makomenaw, 2012). For many Native students attending a TCU, this will most likely be the first and last time they will attend a school in which they are the majority. For students who are accustomed to being around other Native Americans and are apprehensive about attending a NNCU, TCUs are a perfect choice to begin their academic journey.

In addition, 43% of full-time faculty and 46% of faculty at TCUs are Native American (American Indian Higher Education Consortium, 2012). Positive interaction with faculty members has been shown to impact Native American student success (Reeves, 2006). Specifically, Native American TCU students prefer to have access and interaction with Native faculty (Makomenaw, 2012). Moreover, Native students report they receive a high level of support and guidance from Native faculty at TCUs (Ortiz & Heavy Runner, 2003), who serve as mentors to help them navigate through the college environment.

Culture, Language, and Community

TCUs were intentionally developed to be different from mainstream community colleges or four-year NNCUs. The mission of TCUs revolves around inserting Indigenous cultural values into all aspects of the institution. The challenge for TCUs has been blending in cultural knowledge with Western models of education (Boyer, 2005). All TCUs focus on culture and language development in and out of the classroom. Native students who have a robust connection to cultural knowledge have an increased likelihood to succeed in education (Jackson et al., 2003; Rodriguez, 1997). Indigenous languages underpin the cultural tie to community, history, and identity (McCarty & Zepeda, 2006). Students who attend TCUs will have access to traditional culture and language, which help strengthen their cultural identity and further strengthen their community.

In addition to culture and language, TCUs provide access to and infuse the local Native community into the educational experience. A challenge for many Native students in higher education is feeling disconnected between the value of getting an education and being a member of their tribal community (Jackson et al., 2003). Attending a TCU allows students to bridge the value of an education with the roles and responsibilities of being a community member. Moreover, for many students, attending a TCU means having immediate access to family—families are where culture and language is learned. TCUs provide students with the opportunity to attend college while staying connected to their culture, language, family, and community.

TCUs as a Pathway to a Four-Year Degree

Two-year TCUs serve as a great starter institution for Native students looking to transfer to a four-year NNCU or four-year TCU. For some students, the TCU will be the only institution they attend; however, many transfer to a four-year NNCU. A little more than half of TCU students intend on transferring to a four-year NNCU (American Indian College Fund, 2008; Institute for Higher Education Policy, 2006). Thirty-three percent of first-time entering students enrolled in an institution different from their first institution at least once during 2006–2011 (Hossler, Shapiro, & Dundar, 2012). This figure was approximately the same in a separate study conducted by the National Center for Education Statistics (Simone, 2014), where they found 34% of students enrolling in a different institution. In this section, we explore the challenges with assessing the experience and success of TCU students who transfer to four-year institutions. We then examine the role of and need for stronger articulation agreements between two-year TCUs and four-year institutions.

Transfer Rates and Student Pathways Data

Students who attend a TCU prior to attending an NNCU gain confidence while at the TCU (Brown, 2003). Transferring presents challenges, such as adjusting to institutional differences and overcoming stereotypes and ignorance (Makomenaw, 2012). Moreover, the research on TCU transfer students is limited and is often through small qualitative samples. To strengthen access from TCUs to four-year institutions, it is critical to know the myriad paths students take to progress from start to success and the rates at which students succeed. Large-scale data on the success and transfer rates of TCU students are extremely difficult, if not impossible, to find and track. The reason for this lack of data lies in TCU institutional capacity for research and data collection; TCU are typically teaching institutions that do not attract faculty who do research (National Academy of Engineering of the National Academies, 2006). Although the culture of research and institutional data capacity are growing, TCUs are generally behind the curve in producing student-level data that can account for student enrollment through time. Currently, the best options for finding data on TCUs include the National Student Clearinghouse (NSC) and the Integrated Postsecondary Education Data System (IPEDS). Although AIHEC collects and shares data from member TCUs through its annual American Indian Measures of Success (AIHEC-AIMS) data-collection process, the data currently collected are not designed for researching longitudinal student data. One cannot produce, for instance, something as useful as student cohort retention, persistence, or graduation rates from AIHEC-AIMS because it does not include student-level data, only institutional-level data. These types of data are useful for understanding the overall number of students served at TCUs or the types of programs and their enrollment, but they are not useful as we try to come to understand TCU student pathways.

Among the many services that NSC provides to colleges and universities, commercial organizations, and government agencies/programs is access to crucial student-level data needed to describe postsecondary pathways and outcomes, enrollment reporting/verification, and degree verification. More than 3,600 colleges and universities voluntarily report enrollment and degree information to NSC. Ninety-eight percent of all students in public and private U.S. institutions of higher education are represented in the work of NSC (National Student Clearing House, n.d.). NSC provides student-level data, and because the vast majority of student enrollment and degree completion is reported through NSC, its services have the potential to provide a more accurate representation of student pathways and transfer rates.

Currently, 18 out of 34 TCUs are subscribing and submitting student data to NSC or are under contract with NSC to do so in the near future. As a result, TCU enrollment and graduation information is incomplete in the NSC database. Because of the lack of TCU data in the NSC database, TCU student transfer data are not available. No reports on student pathways in the tribal college system can accurately describe the number of students who started at TCUs and may have subsequently transferred to other TCUs or two- and four-year institutions.

Given the relative lack of data in NSC regarding TCU students, we must look elsewhere for supplementary data available at the institution-level. IPEDs reports "transfer-out" rates for individual TCUs. *Transfer-out rates* are defined as the percentage of full-time, first-time students who transferred to another institution. These data provide some sense of the percentage of students moving out of individual TCUs. For the 2014–2015 academic year, only 14 TCUs reported transfer-out rates on IPEDs. Of these, 3 reported transfer-out rates for students who began their studies in the fall of 2007, whereas the remaining 11 reported rates for students who started their studies in the fall of 2010. For the 3 institutions reporting students beginning in 2007, the transfer rates were 3% (United Tribes Technical College), 21% (College of Menominee Nation), and 37% (Diné College). For the 11 reporting the rate for students starting their studies in 2010, the average transfer-out rate was 8.45%.

The data reported in IPEDs are institutional level, not student level, which means the institution is the unit of analysis. As such, the data do not include the educational experiences of students who may have left a TCU and graduated elsewhere. NSC has the potential to assist the TCU system with the types of data it offers. It can provide a way to more accurately formulate a transfer rate and baccalaureate completion rate after transfer. Institutions are often judged heavily on their graduation rates (Burnett, 2013; Lax, 2012; Porter, 2015). Using student-level data and a broader understanding of the pathways that students take to succeed at the postsecondary level can lead to a more detailed understanding of the role TCUs play in the success of students and, hence, answer unfair criticisms that are lobbed their way. Understanding when students transfer from TCUs, the difference earning a pretransfer degree or certificate might have on completing a baccalaureate degree, and the places TCU students transfer (and their subsequent successes) can inform TCUs on how to better serve their students, especially with regard to creating programs to assist students in their transfer to receiving institutions. For example, Monagan and Attewell (2015) indicate one reason that students may not be successful after transfer to a 4-year institution is the loss of credit. As many as 58% of students transferring to a 4-year institution from a 2-year institution do not transfer all or most of their credits to the new institution. The types of data offered through the NSC database could allow for a clearer picture of the myriad pathways that community college students take in their educational pursuits.

Articulation Agreements

The ability for TCU students to attain a four-year degree can be enhanced through mutually beneficial partnerships between TCUs and four-year NNCUs (Guillory, 2013). TCUs understand that their missions are to assist students in training for employment as well as serving as a pipeline for students in completing four-year undergraduate degrees. Articulation agreements have been in place at community colleges since the 1980s to assist students in their efforts to transfer to four-year state institutions.

> Articulation agreements are intended to provide students with more educational options and to remove barriers between community colleges and universities. An articulation agreement, or transfer agreement, is an agreed upon plan between two institutions for credit to be granted from one college to move into a 4-year program at another. By following the transfer agreement plan, in most cases students can take at least half of the required credits toward a Bachelor's degree at Bay Mills Community College and bring those credits with them to their destination institution where they can earn a 4-year degree. (Bay Mills Community College, n.d.)

TCUs offer various forms of articulation agreements. The first are the traditional agreements between TCUs and four-year institutions in specific program areas. For instance, Lac Courte Oreilles Ojibwa Community College holds articulation agreements with the College of St. Scholastica and the Superior and Oshkosh campuses of the University of Wisconsin system for students pursuing a baccalaureate degree in Health Information Management and Human Services, respectively. The second are articulation agreements that encompass all programs at a TCU. Bay Mills Community College has an articulation agreement with Davenport University, whereby all associate degree programs are articulated (Bay Mills Community College, n.d.). The third are statewide agreements that include institutions within that state. Simone (2014) identified five types of state regulations and laws that aim to increase the efficiency with which students can transfer credits: (a) statewide common course numbering systems, (b) statewide articulation agreements among public institutions, (c) standardized general education requirements, (d) mandated acceptance of transfer for specific courses, and (e) policies or guidelines to improve the transfer of credits.

Diné College participates in a program that would fall under the third category called the Arizona General Education Curriculum (AGEC) program. Any student attending Diné College can bypass individual general education course inspection for transferability by completing 1 of 3 AGEC 35 semester credit "blocks." These blocks transfer without loss of credits between Arizona public community colleges or universities in the programs designated by AGEC. TCUs in the state of Montana benefit from the Montana University System, which adopted a common-course numbering system policy. The policy ensures that equivalent courses at different campuses have the same title, number, and prefix. All courses identified in this program are guaranteed to be accepted at the receiving institution. TCUs in the states of Montana, North Dakota, Minnesota, Arizona, Michigan, and Nebraska benefit from such statewide legislation, promoting a smooth transition for transfer students by either identifying courses or standardizing coursework and course numbers among institutions that allow a smooth transition for students wishing to transfer from a TCU to a 4-year institution.

Twelve of the 34 fully accredited TCUs either do not have articulation agreements or do not participate in any of the statewide programs listed previously. No specific articulation agreements exist between TCUs and institutions residing across state lines. However, it may benefit TCU students if TCUs begin assessing the viability of articulation agreements between themselves. TCU students may wish to continue their studies in the TCU system after attaining a 2-year degree/certificate if other TCUs offered 4-year degrees in the same area of study.

To date, no studies have determined the number of TCU students participating in any of these articulation programs. We do not know how successful these programs are in attracting students or actual success rates after transfer. The closest example to describing student success rates occurred in a nursing program partnership between Tohono O'odham Nation and Pima Community College, which highlighted a student success rate of 24%; however, this program did not have an articulation agreement (Campbell, 2007).

Recommendations

TCUs have been successful in recruiting and graduating Native American students at their institutions. Given that most TCUs are two-year institutions, many students will plan on transferring to earn a bachelor's degree. As explained, there is a lack of literature on the success rates and experience of students when transferring to four-year institutions. We offer four recommendations to enhance TCUs as a pathway to a four-year degree.

First, we recommend that four-year institutions strengthen their partnerships with and recruitment of TCU students. The next step is for four-year NNCUs and four-year TCUs to actively recruit these two-year TCU graduates to their institutions. TCUs are a great pathway to a four-year degree for students and offer an opportunity for four-year institutions to increase their Native American student population.

Second, we recommend more research on the experience of TCU transfer students at four-year NNCUs. A few small qualitative studies have been completed on the experience of TCU transfer students; however, more are needed. Some potential areas of research include: How do TCU students make their college transfer choice? Is the experience of a TCU transfer student similar or different depending on the region of the country? Native American students are increasingly choosing the TCU to four-year institution pathway; it is critical to know how to make that transition smooth and successful.

Third, we recommend that all TCUs participate and increase data sharing with NSC. If all TCUs submit enrollment and degree verification data to NSC, then access to student-level data would provide individual TCUs the ability to track students from start to finish. It would allow TCUs the opportunity to understand the pathways that students take from their TCUs and could lead to new program development. For example, trends in the types of degrees students attain after transfer may be exposed in the data. These data can provide a more accurate graduation rate and allow TCUs to calculate transfer rates over time. Moreover, NSC data could provide meaningful comparisons, typically not between the TCU and predominantly NNCUs. Do Native student success rates differ in relation to the type of pathway they take in their educational journeys?

Fourth, we recommend more research on TCU articulation agreements, especially between TCUs. Currently, we do not know the number of students who transfer laterally to other TCU institutions nor do we know the rate at which TCU students move from two-year degree-granting TCUs to four-year degree-granting TCUs; this relatively new phenomenon has yet to be explored. Would TCU students stay within the TCU system if they were able to find their area of study in a four-year degree program at another TCU? More broadly speaking, does the presence of articulation agreements impact TCU transfer rates from TCUs to four-year institutions? Finally, how would articulation rates between TCUs impact overall transfer rates?

Conclusion

In this chapter, we discussed the formation of TCUs, their role in empowering tribal communities, and their role in college access. We discussed how TCUs are affordable, provide social and family support, and offer a predominantly Native environment that enables Native students to succeed. We discussed TCU's role as a pathway to the four-year degree, the advantage of articulation agreements, and the lack of data. Our recommendations included the need for many more articulation agreements, more NSC participation, and more research.

References

Ambler, M. (2005). Tribal colleges redefining success. *Tribal College Journal, 16,* 8–9.

American Indian College Fund. (2008). *American Indian College Fund fact sheet.* Retrieved from www.collegefund.org

American Indian College Fund. (2012). *Fostering success: Need and resiliency among tribal college students.* Retrieved from www.collegefund.org/userfiles/file/FosteringSuccessBRF.pdf

American Indian Higher Education Consortium. (2006). *AIHEC AIMS fact book 2005: Tribal colleges and universities report. Systematic Research, Inc.* Retrieved from www.aihec.org/our-stories/docs/reports/AIHEC_AIMS_FactBook2005.pdf

American Indian Higher Education Consortium. (2012). *2009–2012 AIHEC AIMS fact book: Tribal colleges and universities fact book.* Retrieved from www.aihec.org/resources/documents/AIHEC-AIMSreport_May2012.pdf_

Bay Mills Community College. (n.d.). *Academics: Articulation agreements.* Retrieved from www.bmcc.edu/academics/Articulation/pages/articulation.aspx

Benham, M. K. P., & Stein, W. J. (Eds.). (2003). *The renaissance of American Indian higher education: Capturing the dream.* Mahwah, NJ: Lawrence Erlbaum.

Boyer, P. (2005). To be or not be? TCUs probe identity questions as they "indigenize" their institutions. *Tribal College Journal, 16,* 11–13.

Brayboy, B., Fann, A., Castango, A., & Solyom, J. (2012). Postsecondary education for American Indian and Alaska Natives: Higher education for nation building and self-determination. *ASHE Higher Education Report, 37*(5). Hoboken, NJ: Wiley.

Brown, D. (2003). Tribal colleges: Playing a key role in the transition from secondary to postsecondary education for American Indian students. *Journal of American Indian Education, 42,* 36–45.

Burnett, T. (2013). *The tragedy of tribal colleges.* Retrieved from The James G. Martin Center for Academic Renewal: www.jamesgmartin.center/2013/06/the-tragedy-of-tribal-colleges/

Campbell, A. E. (2007). Retaining American Indian/Alaska Native students in higher education: A case study of one partnership between the Tohono O'odham Nation and Pima County Community College, Tucson, AZ. *Journal of American Indian Education, 46*(2), 19–41.

College Board. (2007). *Federal student aid to undergraduates shows slow growth, while published tuition prices continue to increase.* Retrieved from www.collegeboard.com/press/releases/189547.html

Freeman C., & Fox, M. (2005). Status and trends in the education of American Indians and Alaska Natives (NCES 2005-108). U.S. Department of Education, National Center for Education Statistics. Washington DC: U.S. Government Printing Office. Retrieved from http://nces.ed.gov/pubs2005/2005108.pdf

Guillory, J. (2013). Tribal college collaborations. In H. J. Shotton, S. C Lowe, & S. J. Waterman (Eds.), *Beyond the asterisk: Understanding native students in higher education* (pp. 95–108). Sterling, VA: Stylus.

Guillory, R. M., & Wolverton, M. (2008). It's about family: Native American student persistence in higher education. *The Journal of Higher Education, 79*(1), 58–87.

Hossler, D., Shapiro, D., & Dundar, A. (2012). Signature report 2: Transfer and mobility: A national view of pre-degree student movement in postsecondary institutions. Retrieved from http://nscresearchcenter.org/wp-content/uploads/NSC_Signature_Report_2.pdf

Institute for Higher Education Policy. (2006). *Championing success: A report on the progress of tribal college and university alumni.* Retrieved from www.ihep.org

Jackson, A. P., Smith, S. A., & Hill, C. L. (2003). Academic persistence among Native American college students. *Journal of College Student Development, 44,* 548–565.

Lax, J. (2012). CUNY community college graduation rates do not effectively measure student success. *Thought and Action: The NEA Higher Education Journal, 28,* 118–124.

Makomenaw, M. V. (2012). Welcome to a new world: Experiences of American Indian Tribal College and University transfer students at predominantly White institutions. *International Journal of Qualitative Studies in Education, 25*(7), 855–866.

Makomenaw, M. (2014). Goals, family, and community: What drives tribal college transfer student success. *Journal of Student Affairs Research and Practice, 51*(4), 380–391.

Martin, R. (2005). Serving American Indian students in tribal colleges: Lessons for mainstream colleges. In M. J. T. Fox, S. C. Lowe, & G. S. McClellan (Eds.), *New directions for student services, serving Native American students* (no. 109, pp. 79–86). San Francisco, CA: Jossey-Bass.

McCarty, T. L., & Zepeda, M.E.R.O. (2006). Reclaiming the gift: Indigenous youth counter-narratives on native language loss and revitalization. *The American Indian Quarterly, 30*, 28–48.

Meyer, M. A. (2003). *Ho'oulu our time of becoming: Hawaiian epistemology and early writings.* Honolulu, HI: Ai Pohaku Press.

Monagan, D. B., & Attewell, P. (2015). The community college route to the bachelor's degree. *Educational Evaluation and Policy Analysis, 37*, 70–91.

National Academy of Engineering of the National Academies. (2006). *Engineering studies at tribal colleges and universities.* Washington DC: The National Academies Press.

National Center for Public Policy and Higher Education. (2011). *Affordability and transfer: Critical to increasing baccalaureate degree completion.* Retrieved from www.highereducation.org/reports/pa_at/PolicyAlert_06-2011.pdf

National Student Clearning House. (n.d.). Who we are. Retrieved from www.studentclearinghouse.org/about/

Ortiz, A., & Heavy Runner, I. (2003). Student access, retention, and success: Models of inclusion and support. In M. Benham & W. Stein (Eds.), *The renaissance of American Indian higher education: Capturing the dream* (pp. 215–240). Mahwah, NJ: Lawrence Erlbaum.

Pavel, D. M., & Inglebret, E. (2007). *The American Indian and Alaska Native student's guide to college success.* Westport, CT: Greenwood Press.

Porter, E. (2015, February 7). The promise and failure of community colleges. *The New York Times.* Retrieved from www.nytimes.com/2015/02/18/business/economy/the-promise-and-failure-of-community-colleges.html?_r=0

Reeves, J. J. (2006). *The first-year experience and persistence of Native American Students at one predominantly White institution.* Unpublished master's thesis, Oregon State University.

Reyhner, J., & Eder, J. (2004). *American Indian education: A history.* Norman, OK: University of Oklahoma Press.

Rodriguez, R. (1997). Learning to a live a warrior's life. *Black Issues in Higher Education, 14*, 38–40.

Simone, S. A. (2014). Transferability of postsecondary credit following student transfer or coenrollment. National Center for Educational Statistics. Retrieved from http://nces.ed.gov/pubs2014/2014163.pdf

Tierney, W. G., Sallee, M. W., & Venegas, K. M. (2007). Access and financial aid: American Indian students pay for college. *Journal of College Admission, 197*, 14–23.

U.S. Census Bureau. (2012). The American Indian and Alaska Native population: 2010. *2010 Census briefs*. Retrieved from www.census.gov/prod/cen2010/briefs/c2010br-10.pdf

U.S. Department of Education, National Center for Education Statistics. (2013). Digest of Education Statistics, 2012 (NCES 2014-015), Chapter 3. Retrieved from http://nces.ed.gov/programs/digest/d13/tables/dt13_306.10.asp

Warner, L. S., & Gipp, G. E. (2009). *Tradition and culture in the millennium: Tribal colleges and universities*. Charlotte, NC: Information Age.

4

NATIVE STUDENT FINANCIAL AID AS NATIVE NATION BUILDING

History, Politics, and Realities

Christine A. Nelson (Diné and Laguna Pueblo)
and Amanda R. Tachine (Navajo)

Through a Native nation-building lens, we challenge the notion that financial aid for Native students should solely be defined as monetary funding that provides college access and persistence. In this chapter, we claim that financial aid for Native students contributes to Native nation-building capacity, and to develop this claim, we analyze the historical, political, and societal factors impacting financial aid. We contextualize Native higher education history and aid within the dominant financial aid history to highlight intersecting factors often excluded from the financial aid discussion for Native students. This chapter concludes by offering recommendations to institutions of higher education and tribal nations to best serve Native students at the intersection of financial aid and college access and persistence.

> Something that's not even on the radar of most people is that tribes are actually sovereign nations, that the misunderstanding that native people are not just a racial group, but we're also a political group because we are citizens of sovereign nations . . . we're lumped in with other groups but our issues are different. . . . And then I think there are the everyday stereotypes and misconceptions about what comes free for native people. So, the misperception that native students go to college for free. . . . And, it's a confusion of the trust responsibility of the federal government when it comes to education as a part of our treaty rights and what was negotiated in treaties with tribes in the United States government in exchange for lands that were ceded. (Shotton, 2016)

Educational leaders have emphasized the distinct political relationship that Native nations have with the United States, thus indicating the government's financial investment and obligation for Native education. A precedence that spans over the past 500 years has been stated in congressional documents: "Federal provision of educational services and assistance to Indian children is based not on race/ethnicity but primarily on their membership in, eligibility for membership in, or familial relationship to members of Indian tribes, which are political entities" (Congressional Research Service, 2015, p. 1). In the higher education context, interrogating the history and policies of financial aid provides a deeper understanding and awareness of the unique relationship between Native college students and federal financial aid.

This chapter centers the political relationship between tribal nations and the federal government to begin addressing the misconception surrounding Native student financial aid. As former college students and student affairs practitioners, we frequently hear the false rhetoric involving Native students and how they pay for college. One common misconception we hear is that college is free for all Native students. Empirical evidence shows that Native students do not go to college for free (Goldrick-Rab, 2016; Nelson, 2015a). To add to that conversation, we think one of the root causes of these misconceptions is the exclusion of political status and sovereignty within the financial aid discourse.

We also realize that Native students are talking about financial cost in ways unaccounted for in the higher education literature and contrary to societal misconceptions (e.g., "Natives go to college for free"). Tribal funding as "Native Nation Building" (Brayboy, Fann, Castagno, & Solyom, 2012; Nelson, 2015b) and sociocultural conditions (Tachine, 2015) profoundly shapes college affordability and students' degree pursuits. To unravel these complex concepts, we understand that history, at the intersection of federal, state, and tribal policy and the socioeconomic maladies facing Native communities, influence current Native college students' financial experiences. This chapter ties together these concepts and provides a discussion about financial aid by first exploring how Native students are currently paying for college. We then briefly describe how we use Native nation building (NNB) to expand on our understanding of Native student financial aid. We then unpack the historical, political, and current societal factors pertinent to understanding Native student financial aid. We conclude with recommendations on strengthening the Native student financial aid discourse.

Native Students Paying for College

Research provides information on the multifaceted influences of financial aid on students' college choice (Perna, 2008), students' perceptions of the cost of college (Heller, 1997; Perna, 2010), and students' persistence to graduation (DesJardins & McCall, 2010; Dynarski, 2003). Undoubtedly, financial aid is an important aspect of the college-going process, but little research specifically explores Native student experiences with paying for college (Mendez & Mendez, 2013; Mendez, Mendoza, & Malcolm, 2011; Nelson, 2015b; Tierney, Sallee, & Venegas, 2007). Currently, Native students in the United States, like other college students, have access to federal financial aid sources such as Pell Grants, Supplemental Educational Opportunity Grants, Teacher Education Assistance for College and Higher Education grants, and work study. They also have access to state financial aid sources and institutional financial aid. Several private or nonprofit financial aid sources, such as the Gates Millennium Scholars Program, the American Indian College Fund (AICG), the American Indian Graduate Center (AIGC), and the Cobell Scholarship, specifically target funding for American Indian and Alaska Native students. Last, tribally enrolled students may also have access to specific financial aid and scholarships offered by their tribe.

The National Postsecondary Student Aid Survey (2004 & 2012) presents some interesting trends in the Native student financial aid profile (Nelson, 2015a). For example, 87% of Native college students received financial aid in 2012, an increase of 10% since 2004. Although that percentage is high, closer examination of those who are funded and the average dollars awarded paints another picture. Nearly half (46%) of Native college students were first-generation, low-income[1] students, an increase of 82% since 2004. Moreover, the average need-based aid awarded to American Indian and Alaskan Native students is $4,334. As tuition increases across the nation, $4,334 is not enough for most in-state tuition costs. In 2016–2017, the College Board (2016) reported that the average tuition and fee costs for in-state undergraduate students at public 4-year institutions ranged from $5,060 (Wyoming) to $15,650 (New Hampshire). Furthermore, Native college students received the lowest amount of aid compared with all student racial/ethnic groups (Aud, Fox, & KewalRamani, 2010; Nelson, 2015a). Juxtaposing the low amount of aid received with the high percentage of recipients furthers the argument that Native student financial aid needs to be scrutinized.

Framing Native Student Financial Aid

In this chapter, we utilize NNB (Brayboy et al., 2012) to critically analyze the concept of financial aid and to provide a more complete discussion on financial aid for Native student populations. An NNB model seeks to promote a holistic approach to understand, promote, and build tribal capacity within individual tribal communities (Brayboy et al., 2012). NNB, at the intersection of financial aid, allows us to understand how the concept of aid impacts the educational landscape in both the historical and modern contexts. Ultimately, NNB allows us to analyze the purpose and function of financial aid to develop a more complete narrative surrounding Native students and aid.

Native student financial aid honors and acknowledges the exchange of Native land for the protection of Native peoples as cited in numerous treaty agreements between Native nations and the U.S. government (Deloria & Lytle, 1983). The modern context of Native students receiving financial aid is linked with societal and historical factors, urging the point that Native student financial aid is cyclical and holistic. Native student financial aid as NNB is defined as a relationship rooted in treaty agreements and fundamentally tied to the belief that higher education is connected to the betterment of Native nations. To begin describing this relationship, the next section contextualizes Native higher education within the dominant financial aid history to further explain how the political status of tribal communities is germane to today's financial aid discourse.

Historic and Socioeconomic Context of Native Student Financial Aid

Crucial to our work is understanding the historical implications of financial aid on the modern financial aid context for Native students. In this section, we elaborate on the history of Native higher education through a financial aid lens to assert that financial aid for today's Native students is entangled within a national historic and political context that is relevant to their current experiences.

From a dominant U.S. perspective, financial aid has been framed as federal, state, institutional, and private funding sources that provide college access, leading to individualized benefits in terms of degree completion, career opportunities, and monetary wealth (Baum, Ma, & Payea, 2013; Bidwell, 1989; Day & Newburger, 2002). We contend that the most commonly held definition of *financial aid* is money received by a student to alleviate the costs of attending postsecondary education. Simply stated by the Federal Student Aid (FSA) website, *student financial aid* is "money to help pay for college or career school" (Federal Student Aid, n.d.). This definition dilutes our understanding of financial aid. When we only view aid as money for a student to attend college, we overlook financial aid as part of a larger and deeper network that stems from historical policy influenced by unique political relationships between Native nations and the U.S. government.

With an NNB lens, we frame financial aid, from as early as the 1500s, as a phenomenon experiencing different phases of intent and impact. Thus, the intent and impact of providing educational access through various funding sources may or may not have served the best interest of a Native person or his or her community. To be clear, financial aid for Native student college access is of importance, but as we continue to investigate ways to overcome educational attainment barriers, we must acknowledge the complex implications embedded within the historical intent of Native student financial aid.

Tethering Relationship: Historical Treaties and Policies Linked to Financial Aid for Native Peoples

On colonial contact, educational initiatives and funding, including higher education, were used as a strategy to either remove Native students physically and psychologically from their tribal communities and sense of being or to discredit Indigenous knowledges as a viable form of education (Wright, 1988). From the 1500s to the turn of the twentieth century, funding allocated toward Native education was paternalistic in nature and used as a tool to convert Natives to Eurocentric White society. Whereas monetary contributions came from the U.S. government, missionary donors in England provided colonial colleges with financial support to educate Native students (Carney, 1999).

Three of the original 9 colonial colleges came to view Native education as a potential funding opportunity and rewrote their charters to include an emphasis on educating Native students in Eurocentric knowledge. For example, Harvard college, which was struggling financially soon after being founded in 1636, rewrote its charter in 1650 to include "the education of the English and Indian youth of this country in knowledge and godliness" (Carney, 1999, p. 1). Donors, such as the Boyle fund, an endowment created by a British scientist, gave Harvard 200 pounds and an additional 45 pounds yearly specifically for Native education (Carney, 1999). In return for funding from the English Society for the Propagation of the Bible in New England, Harvard agreed to waive tuition and provide housing to American Indian students in its first brick building, the Harvard Indian College (Peabody Museum of Anthropology and Ethnology, n.d.). Although the intent was to increase Native student participation in Eurocentric higher education, degree completion was dismal. Only 5 Native students ever attended Harvard between 1660 and 1714, and the Indian College only stood for 15 years before being destroyed so the bricks could be used for other purposes. Of the 5 Native men who attended Harvard during this early colonial era, only 1 was awarded a degree just months before succumbing to consumption. Three others also died before graduating, 2 to illness and 1 in a shipwreck. The fifth left Harvard to become a Mariner (Peabody Museum of Anthropology and Ethnology, n.d.).

Aid for non-Natives attending colonial colleges was also influenced by the European university system. Higher education, which predominantly served White males, was funded by the student, the church, minimal governmental subsidies, and philanthropic contributions from wealthy families (Fuller, 2014). Although their funding streams were similar in nature, the purpose in attending college for Natives and non-Natives was not. The function of Westernized higher education for Native students was to assimilate them into White society (Carney, 1999). For non-Native populations, higher education promoted elitism, knowledge production, and future theologians (Fuller, 2014).

At the turn of the nineteenth century, higher education funding began to shift. Westward expansion naturally led to the establishment of colleges and universities in the West. However, the American Revolutionary War impacted higher education by diverting funding from education to military functions (Fuller, 2014), affecting both Native (Carney, 1999) and non-Native student populations. White students began to rely more heavily on philanthropic donations for funding, and to maintain access to college, the first system of financial aid emerged. Harvard College in particular began the first formal system for determining student need, which eventually led to offering zero-interest student loans primarily for poor white male students (Fuller, 2014). For Native communities, the war and western expansion threatened Indian territories, which ultimately intensified the U.S. government's assimilation efforts (Carney, 1999). During the American Revolutionary War, the U.S. government had a strong desire to acquire more land, which led to funding educational practices that "were designed to train Indians for subservience, making them amenable not only to surrendering tribal lands but also to entering the manual/domestic labor market" (Lomawaima & McCarty, 2006, p. 49).

Following the American Revolutionary War, the U.S. government and individual tribal nations entered into treaty agreements. These treaties established a trust relationship, where the U.S. government, in trade for appropriating land, became responsible for the social well-being of Native peoples (Adams, 1995). Among a combination of other trust responsibilities, access to Eurocentric-based education was included in treaty agreements. According to Newton (2012) between the years 1794 and 1871, more than 150 treaties were signed between tribal nations and the U.S. government, providing individual tribes with teachers, schools, and other support services to promote academic and/or vocational training (as cited in Congressional Research Service, 2015, p. 2).

The federal government's intent to invest money in Native education was to increase western expansion and was rooted in a strategy to assimilate Native peoples to Eurocentric ways of life. The production of Native knowledge and Native scholars/leaders was not a goal. By 1838, federal funds were funneled to 93 schools where approximately 3,700 Native students were served (Rockwell, 2010). The motto originating in the 1860s and 1870s during the Indian Wars, "The only good Indian is a dead Indian" (Nabokov, 1993, as cited in Carney, 1999, p. 65), soon became, "Save the Man . . . Kill the Indian" (Pratt, 1892, p. 47). The latter message illustrated Eurocentric ideals for the education of Native people and guided the beliefs of many boarding school proponents (Adams, 1995). For Native communities, the boarding school era was a dark time. Many children's lives were met with trauma, illness, and death (Child, 1998).

On transitioning into the 1900s, the federal government commissioned two reports on the status of the country's Indian nations: the Merriam Report in 1928 and the Kennedy Report of 1969. These reports looked closely at the social and educational conditions facing tribal communities while also documenting inhumane Eurocentric practices in schools and communities. Both reports brought attention to the challenges that Native students faced in schools and provided benchmarks that clearly showed a glaring lack of educational progress over a 40-year period in tribal communities (Meriam et al., 1928; Special Subcommittee on Indian Education, 1969). By the mid-1950s, public awareness of Native rights and wellness increased, and individual tribal nation involvement became more prevalent, and yet federal control proliferated, and many policies remained rooted in assimilation tactics (Lomawaima & McCarty, 2006). Public Law 959: The Indian Adult Vocational Training Act of 1956 was a good example of how paternalistic methods of assimilation were met by tribal self-determination in education. This law targeted young tribal members, providing opportunities to leave tribal communities and relocate with their families to urban cities, such as Chicago, Denver, Los Angeles, New York, and the San Francisco-Oakland Bay areas. By the end of 1957, the federal government spent $6 million to relocate 20,433 Natives (Ono, 2004).

This relocation program emphasized postsecondary vocational training, not higher education (Carney, 1999), and the trade skills obtained by participating young Native adults led to employment in cities, creating a culture that emphasized financial independence and urbanism. The implications and impacts of the program are rife with complexities because it separated these young Native adults from their tribal communities. On the one hand, "The [relocation] program was a simple process in which the BIA [Bureau of Indian Affairs] offered one-way tickets to jobs or training in a selected set of cities" (Willard, 1997, p. 30). On the other hand, the relocation program "strengthened . . . pan-Indian identity and created a support system which would substitute for reservations" (Ono, 2004, p. 27). Clearly, postsecondary education and job training through the relocation programs were another attempt by the federal government to expedite assimilation by severing ties to and reducing populations on Indigenous territories.

Subsequent to the relocation program, the federal government created policies and laws to address the concerns of returning war veterans. The Servicemen's Readjustment Act of 1944, or the GI Bill, increased college access for military personnel and veterans at unprecedented rates. However, the early years of the GI Bill only increased inequities between marginalized populations and the White middle class (Herbold, 1994–1995). It was not until civil rights leaders advocated for the desegregation of schools and demanded policy changes to improve access to quality education that access to higher education became more of a reality for all (Wallenstein, 2008).

The GI Bill was one of the few nationwide policies that directly benefited Native communities (Redhouse, 2016). The Kennedy Report of 1969, along with social movements such as the American Indian Movement in the mid-1960s and 1970s, influenced federal policymakers to become more aware of the social conditions on tribal lands and the need for the federal government to honor treaty trust responsibilities by shifting away from paternalistic practices and moving toward supporting tribal capacity building (Carney, 1999). Notable policy changes included the passage of the 1971 Navajo Community College Act and the 1978 Tribally Controlled Community College Act. For the first time, tribes were given the freedom to self-determine their higher educational initiatives. Coupled with the Indian Self-Determination and Educational Assistance Act of 1975, tribal nations began making college access for their tribal members a reality on their own terms.

Developing Relationship: Tribal Self-Determination and Local Control

After centuries enduring an educational system where funding was used to dismantle tribal communities, the modern Native higher education climate is embracing self-determination and NNB more than ever. In the twenty-first century, Native student financial aid is becoming more complex. Aid is viewed as an obligation to and recognition of past treaty agreements, as well as a tool to reclaim and rebuild tribal ways of knowing and long-term tribal sustainability for NNB (Brayboy et al., 2012; Nelson, 2015a, 2015b). We focus on two avenues related to college affordability to emphasize this point:

(a) tribal college and university (TCU) fiscal practices and (b) tribal financial aid and scholarships.

Tribal College and University Fiscal Practices

As of 2017, there are 37 TCUs with specific goals to serve tribal communities. The National Center for Education Statistics Integrated Postsecondary Education Data System reports that TCUs serve nearly 28,000 students.[2] TCUs epitomize what it means to self-determine education because they are structured to build capacity that is culturally relevant and respectful to individual tribes (Stein, 2009). Much like the 567 sovereign tribal nations across the United States, each TCU has a unique student population, institutional culture, and academic focus. A common challenge they share is institutional funding. TCUs are ineligible to receive state and local funds from tax contributions, which financially strains their ability to operate at full capacity (Nelson & Frye, 2016). Moreover, the Tribally Controlled College or University Assistance Act of 1978 authorized $8,000 of federal support per student attending TCUs, but in 2014, the actual federal allocation to tribal college was $6,335 per enrolled student (Nelson & Frye, 2016).

Despite ongoing financial strife, maintaining community needs and individual college access is at the heart of a TCU's mission. This commitment is arguably a direct reflection of tribal self-determination and NNB. In 2010, the American Indian Higher Education Consortium (AIHEC) reported that 19,070 full- and part-time students were served by TCUs and, "through community-based education and support programs," nearly 47,000 community members (American Indian Higher Education Consortium, 2012, p. 3). Furthermore, TCUs' duty to provide affordable college to their students is demonstrated when comparing tuition and student loan practices to mainstream institutions. For example, it is common to see mainstream institutions, under fiscal challenges, raise tuition to offset budgetary shortcomings (Hemelt & Marcotte, 2011; Koshal & Koshal, 2010). TCUs have avoided raising tuition (American Indian Higher Education Consortium, 2012; Nelson & Frye, 2016) and, in some cases, have actually forgiven outstanding tuition bills to ensure students are able to continue their education (Billy, 2014).

A majority of TCUs have also opted to not participate in federal student loan programs. Non-Native colleges and universities have increased student loan participation and amounts as a cost-sharing practice (Johnstone, 2005) that has been linked to the rising costs of tuition (Lucca, Nadauld, & Shen, 2016). TCU leaders believe that by not participating in student loan programs, they are promoting healthier financial futures for their students by not boosting educational debt (American Indian College Fund, 2002; American

Indian Higher Education Consortium, 2012). Systematically, TCUs' continued nonparticipation in student loan programs further helps college access for Native students in terms of keeping tuition rates reasonable. Ultimately, TCU financial aid policies and practices underscore self-determination and diverge from mainstream institutions to ensure that financial aid practices and policies best serve their students and tribal community.

Tribal Financial Aid and Scholarships

Originating in the 1950s, *tribal financial aid* is defined as tribal funds allocated to enrolled tribal members to offset the cost of attending a postsecondary institution (Carney, 1999). Prior to the development of TCUs, tribal members seeking a higher education attended mainstream institutions, such as a local community college or state institution. Nelson (2018) asserts that the use of tribal funds for student aid reflects the values of NNB as many tribes with tribal higher education departments invest in a tribal member's education with the hope that the student will contribute back to the tribe following degree completion. Although we use the blanket term *tribal financial aid and scholarships*, it is important to note that (a) not all tribes have the capacity to offer funding for their tribal members, and (b) each tribal nation self-determines the administration of such awards (Nelson, 2018).

Fuller (2014) stated there is a change in national financial aid funding practices, which are going "from local, mostly philanthropic efforts, to a nationwide system of aid, interconnected and responsive to changes in American higher education and society" (p. 42). Whereas Eurocentric-based higher education for Native communities emerged from an elaborate system to eradicate Native ways of knowing and living, Native higher education is returning to local, philanthropic efforts (Brayboy et al., 2012), with tribal self-determination and NNB at its core. Tribal financial aid and scholarships reflect this localized effort by serving their citizens, with the hope that tribal scholarship recipients will reciprocate the tribe's financial investment in education by returning to tribal nations and communities to enact positive change. By asserting their voices in higher education through student financial aid, it can be expected that tribal financial aid will directly impact a larger Native population by promoting local capacity building and sustainability.

To best serve today's Native students, it is critical to understand the historical intentions of financial aid while recognizing the differences between mainstream financial aid and Native student financial aid. Many Native students have one or two generations of family members that attended boarding schools, participated in relocation programs, or received the first waves of tribal financial aid and scholarships. By articulating Native student financial aid from a historical perspective to current reality, we can see how Native higher education has evolved; yet even from that vantage point, the picture is still incomplete. As we uncover financial aid trends and frame Native student financial aid as NNB, it becomes difficult to disentangle the sociocultural realities of Native people today from this discussion. The current sociocultural context, which includes factors such as poverty and unemployment, penetrate the livelihood and educational attainment of today's Native populations.

Sociocultural Context Shaping Native Peoples

Important aspects of the Native experiences, often unexamined in higher education research, are the sociocultural contexts that shape Native livelihoods. According to the 2010 U.S. Census, 5.2 million people identified as American Indian and Alaskan Native. At the time of this book's printing, 567 American Indian and Alaskan Native tribes are federally recognized. Moreover, 334 Native reservations are federally and state recognized, with roughly 22% of Natives living within those reservation boundaries (U.S. Census Bureau, 2011). The states with the highest Native populations are overwhelmingly rural (National Rural Assembly, 2011), and according to the 2010 U.S. Census, the 10 states with the lowest population densities also have high Native populations (National Rural Assembly, 2011).

Native peoples who live in rural reservation towns deal with significantly scarcer business opportunities when compared with other towns. For example, the Navajo nation (the largest reservation in the United States) is comparable in size to the state of West Virginia. In 2014, West Virginia had 90,403 businesses within its boundaries (personal communication, Office of the West Virginia Secretary of State, April 4, 2013). As of 2010, there were only 636 businesses within the entire Navajo reservation (Division of Economic Development, 2010). That stark contrast paints a striking picture of the business development differences within land areas of the same size.

Several factors influence the lack of enterprises on reservations. One reason is land. Most of the land on Native reservations is held in trust by the federal government due to treaty stipulations mentioned earlier. Because Natives do not own their land, they cannot use the land to build equity or finance a business. Another reason for the scarcity of businesses on Native lands is the possibility of dual taxation through state and tribal taxes, which discourages many businesses from opening or starting enterprises. Politics and the amount of time required for approval to start a business on Native land also hinder increasing business establishments on reservations.

Connected to sparse businesses are high rates of poverty and unemployment. In 2014, at the national level, the median household income for Native populations was $39,715 compared with $56,746 for non-Natives. The 2014 unemployment rates suggest another depressed economic scenario. The average unemployment rate for Native populations was 12.4%, which is double the national rate of 6.1% (U.S. Executive Office of the President, 2014).

Further complicating the livelihood among Native people is a lack of basic living needs. Eleven percent of Native households lack kitchen facilities, 12% lack plumbing, and 17% lack telephone services (National Rural Assembly, 2011). In a recent report, 14% of Native homes in Arizona had no electricity, compared with less than 1.5% of non-Native households (Mariella, Clashin, & Williams, 2011). Specifically, among the Navajo people living on the Navajo reservation, approximately 16,000 households do not have electricity (Shone, 2010), and 40% of homes do not have running water (Conover, 2013). These sociocultural realities of Native students do not cease to exist when they enter higher education, and by continuing to explore Native student financial aid as NNB, we can better understand how paying for college is more than receiving money to attend college.

Strengthening the Native Student Financial Aid Discourse: Thoughts and Recommendations

In this chapter, we frame financial aid for Native students as NNB. The political relationship between sovereign Native nations and the federal government is a fundamental key to understanding Native financial aid today. Unfortunately, this relationship is rooted in systemic racism that sought to assimilate and eradicate Native cultures and ways of life. The paternalistic educational initiatives supported by the U.S. government and early churches fundamentally shaped and continue to shape the socioeconomic challenges that Native communities face. These factors broaden conversations surrounding college affordability. The more we scrutinize the multifaceted nature of financial aid, the better we can articulate the realities of Native students' ability to pay for college.

Tribal nations are currently confronting the costs of higher education for their members by operating tribal colleges and providing tribal financial aid. Yet more work is needed to strengthen the financial aid relationship among the federal government, institutions of higher education, and Native nations. Non-Native colleges and universities (NNCUs) can take several steps to strengthen the Native student financial aid discourse. The first three recommendations are procedural in nature, whereas the fourth supports statewide cooperation among several entities and institutions. First, we recommend institutions be informed and knowledgeable of Native student financial aid. For example, both authors attended colleges with financial aid coordinator(s) who understood Native student financial aid and its implications from an individual student level as well as a broader tribal level. Having more than one person who is familiar with Native student financial aid is critical. This allows the consistent availability of an expert in this field. Relying on one staff member to understand and share critical information related to Native student financial aid resources only complicates the process for students and overburdens the individual staff member assigned to this duty.

Our second recommendation is to collect information on the tribal affiliation(s) of Native students enrolled in your institution. The political intentions of the U.S. government during early colonization and the treaties signed with tribal nations for ceded lands make Native students political entities. Given this political significance, identifying the tribal affiliation(s) of students is a necessary step toward supporting Native college students and demonstrates an institution's commitment to valuing tribal identity and the tribal communities students come from. By recording tribal identity, institutions can build a more nuanced understanding of tribal institutional representation and can begin to map out enrollment, retention, and graduation patterns for particular tribal nations. The fact that tribal nations are sovereign nations should encourage all college leaders and administrators to position tribal nations equally with other federal and state agencies. We suggest that institutions consult with tribes to garner an understanding of how current reporting mechanisms directed toward state and federal agencies can be replicated for Native students attending their institutions.

As an extension to including tribal affiliation in student information systems, our third recommendation is to keep track of and document money received from tribal nations to look for patterns of funding received and to further understand the implications of tribal financial aid on student college-going trends (e.g., enrollment, graduation, GPA). For example, Nelson's (2015b) study found that among the 37 Native students who applied for tribal financial aid, the collective amount of aid filtered through their higher education institutions amounted to approximately $150,000 annually. In Nelson's study, participating institutions did not differentiate tribal financial aid from other external entities providing student financial support. Rather, tribal financial aid was flagged as a third-party scholarship and could not be further disaggregated. The inability to accurately measure which Native students are receiving tribal financial aid further limits an institution's ability to empirically measure student-level data. This lack of data directly impacts both the institution and tribal nations and their abilities to better support Native students through graduation.

For our fourth recommendation, we find it important to implement a statewide tribal consultation policy that establishes principles governing interactions among higher education institutions and tribal nations. Arizona State University, Northern Arizona University, University of Arizona, the

Inter-Tribal Council of Arizona, and the Navajo Nation developed a single, mutually acceptable tribal consultation policy. In 2016, the Arizona Board of Regents (ABOR) approved a policy that outlines consultation as well as communication principles between the state higher education institutions and tribal nations on issues such as land use, educational policy, and research. ABOR chair Heiler stated, "This is an important policy that clarifies and strengthens relations with tribal nations and Arizona's public universities. This policy will guide interactions with Arizona's tribes and provide a working framework on which we build future projects and initiatives with Native nations" (Arizona Board of Regents, 2016, p. 2). Establishing a tribal consultation policy is a promising step for building systemic avenues for higher education institutions to strengthen relationships with Native nations.

Conclusion

By relying on perspectives that do not consider the unique historical, political, and socioeconomic factors impacting funding and financial aid for Native students, NNCUs continue to inadequately serve this student population, and misnomers, such as Natives go to college for free, continue unchallenged. In this chapter, we contextualized the history of Native student financial aid by triangulating it with several points of time in financial aid history. By viewing financial aid for Native students as Native nation building, we can see how the history of financial aid and educational initiatives impact students today. As financial aid and higher educational initiatives begin to further support capacity building for tribal nations, now is the time for tribal nations and higher education institutions to pay more thorough attention to Native student experiences with financial aid. Despite more than 500 years of colonization and a significant amount of resources put toward assimilation efforts through education, Native people have resisted and persisted in higher education. Further exploration on the role of financial aid for Native student college access, persistence, and graduation is warranted. We hope this chapter acts as a catalyst to further this conversation.

Notes

1. *First generation, low income* is defined by TRIO standards. First generation indicates student does not have a parent with a college degree. Low income indicates student comes from a family with a household income lower than $25,000.

2. Derived by authors using IPEDS Data Center from the IPEDS 12-month unduplicated headcount at TCUs (AY 2012–2013). This figure does not include Comanche Nation, Muscogee Nation, and Wind River.

References

Adams, D. W. (1995). *Education for extinction: American Indians and the boarding school experience, 1875–1928.* Lawrence, KS: University Press of Kansas.

American Indian College Fund. (2002). *Cultivating success: The critical value of American Indian scholarships and the positive impact of tribal college capital construction.* Denver, CO: The American Indian College Fund. Retrieved from www.collegefund.org/userfiles/file/CultivatingSuccess.pdf

American Indian Higher Education Consortium. (2012). *2009–2010 AIHEC AIMS fact book: Tribal colleges and universities report.* Alexandria, VA: Author. Retrieved from www.aihec.org/our-stories/docs/reports/AIHEC_AIMSreport_May2012.pdf

Arizona Board of Regents. (2016). *New tribal consultation policy approved by ABOR.* Retrieved from www.azregents.edu/sites/default/files/news-releases/New%20Tribal%20Consultation%20Policy%20Approved%20by%20ABOR%20.pdf

Aud, S., Fox, M., & KewalRamani, A. (2010). *Status and trends in the education of racial and ethnic groups* (NCES 2010-015). U.S. Department of Education, National Center for Education Statistics. Washington DC: U.S. Government Printing Office.

Baum, S., Ma, J., & Payea, K. (2013). *Education pays.* New York: College Board.

Bidwell, C. A. (1989). The meaning of educational attainment. *Research in the Sociology of Educational and Socialization, 8,* 117–138.

Billy, C. (2014, May 1). Tribal colleges doing more with less (M. Martin, Interviewer). *Paying for college.* [Audio File]. Retrieved from www.npr.org/2014/05/01/308619966/tribal-colleges-do-more-with-less

Brayboy, B. M. J., Fann, A. J., Castagno, A. E., & Solyom, J. A. (2012). Postsecondary education for American Indian and Alaskan Natives: Higher education for nation building and self-determination. *ASHE Higher Education Report, 37*(5). Hoboken, NJ: Wiley.

Carney, C. M. (1999). *Native American higher education in the United States.* New Brunswick, NJ: Transaction Publishers.

Child, B. (1998). *Boarding school seasons: American Indian families, 1900–1940.* Lincoln, NE: University of Nebraska Press.

College Board. (2016). *Trends in higher education: Tuition and fees by sector and state over time.* Retrieved from https://trends.collegeboard.org/college-pricing/figures-tables/tuition-fees-sector-state-over-time

Congressional Research Service. (2015). *Indian elementary-secondary education: Programs, background, and issues.* CRS-RL34205. Retrieved from www.crs.gov/pages/Reports.aspx?PRODCODE=RL34205

Conover, C. (2013, April 26). Running water: Not taken for granted [Web log post]. Retrieved from http://support.devel.azpm.org/s/14545-looking-for-water/

Day, J. C., & Newburger, E. C. (2002). *The big payoff: Education attainment and synthetic estimates of work-life earnings.* Special Studies Report. Washington DC: U.S. Department of Commerce.

Deloria, V., & Lytle, C. M. (1983). *American Indians, American justice* (1st ed.) Austin, TX: University of Texas Press.

DesJardin, S. L., & McCall, B. P. (2010). Simulating the effects of financial aid packages on college student stopout, reenrollment spells, and graduation chances. *The Review of Higher Education, 33*(4), 513–541.

Division of Economic Development. (2010). *2009-2010 comprehensive economic development strategy. The Navajo Nation.* Retrieved from www.navajobusiness.com/pdf/CEDS/CED_NN_Final_09_10.pdf

Dynarski, S. (2003). Does aid matter? Measuring the effect of student aid on college attendance and completion. *American Economic Review, 93*(1), 279–288.

Federal Student Aid. (n.d.). *Types of aid.* Retrieved from http://studentaid.ed.gov/sa/types

Fuller, M. B. (2014). A history of financial aid to students. *Journal of Student Aid, 44*(1), 42–68.

Goldrick-Rab, S. (2016). *Paying the price.* Chicago, IL: University of Chicago Press.

Heller, D. (1997). Student price response in higher education: An update to Leslie and Brinkman. *Journal of Higher Education, 68*(6), 624–659.

Hemelt, S. W., & Marcotte, D. E. (2011). The impact of tuition increases on enrollment at public colleges and universities. *Educational Evaluation and Policy Analysis, 33*(4), 435–457.

Herbold, H. (1994–1995, Winter). Never a level playing field: Blacks and the GI bill. *The Journal of Blacks in Higher Education, 6*(105), 104–108.

Johnstone, D. B. (2005, May). Higher educational accessibility and financial viability: The role of student loans. Paper presented at the World Report on Higher Education: The Financing of Universities II International Barcelona Conference on Higher Education, Global University Network for Innovation (GUNI), Barcelona, Spain.

Koshal, R. K., & Koshal, M. (2010). State appropriations and higher education tuition: What is the relationship? *Education Economics, 8*(1), 81–89.

Lomawaima, K. T., & McCarty, T. L. (2006). *To remain an Indian: Lessons in democracy from a century of Native American education.* New York, NY: Teachers College Press.

Lucca, D. O., Nadauld, T., & Shen, K. (2016). *Credit supply and the rise in college tuition: Evidence from the expansion in federal student aid programs.* Staff report no. 733. Federal Reserve Bank of New York. Retrieved from www.newyorkfed.org/medialibrary/media/research/staff_reports/sr733.pdf

Mariella, P., Clashin, T., & Williams, S. (2011). Tribes and energy within Arizona. In C. Miller & S. Moore (Eds.), *Arizona's energy future: Background report prepared by Arizona State University.* Retrieved from http://aztownhall.org/Resources/Documents/99th_Background_Report.pdf

Mendez, J., & Mendez, J. (2013). Student perceptions of American Indian financial aid. *Journal of American Indian Education, 52*(1), 45–64.

Mendez, J. P., Mendoza, P., & Malcolm, Z. (2011). The impact of financial aid on Native American students. *Journal of Diversity in Higher Education, 4*(1), 12–25.

Meriam, L., Brown, R. A., Roe Cloud, H., Dale, E. E., Duke, E., Edwards, H. R., … Spillman, W. J. (1928). *The problem of Indian administration.* Report of a survey made at the request of honorable Hubert Work, Secretary of the Interior, and submitted to him February 1, 1928. Retrieved from http://files.eric.ed.gov/fulltext/ED087573.pdf

National Rural Assembly. (2011). *Innovative Native nations in rural America.* National Congress of American Indians. Retrieved from www.fourbands.org/downloads/Tribal_Policy_Paper_HighRez.pdf

Nelson, C. A. (2015a). *American Indian/Alaskan Natives in higher education fact sheet. Center for Policy Research and Strategy Post-Traditional Student Profiles.* Washington DC: American Council on Education. Retrieved from www.acenet.edu/news-room/Documents/Higher-Ed-Spotlight-American-Indians-and-Alaska-Natives-in-Undergraduate-Education.pdf

Nelson, C. A. (2015b). American Indian college students as Native nation builders: Tribal financial aid as a lens for understanding college-going paradox. Unpublished doctoral dissertation, University of Arizona, Tucson, AZ.

Nelson, C. A. (2018). The intersection of paying for college and tribal sovereignty: Exploring native college student experiences with tribal financial aid. In R. S. Minthorn & H. J. Shotton (Eds.), *Reclaiming Indigenous research in higher education* (pp. 146–161). New Brunswick, NJ: Rutgers University Press.

Nelson, C. A., & Frye, J. R. (2016). *Tribal colleges and university funding: Tribal sovereignty at the intersection of federal, state, and local funding.* Issue brief. Washington DC: American Council on Education.

Newton, N. J. (Ed.). (2012). *Cohen's handbook of federal Indian law.* San Francisco, CA: LexisNexis.

Ono, A. (2004). The relocation and employment assistance programs, 1948–1970: Federal Indian policy and the early development of the Denver Indian community. *Indigenous Nations Studies Journal, 5*(1), 27–50.

Peabody Museum of Anthropology and Ethnology. (n.d.). *The Harvard Indian College.* Retrieved from www.peabody.harvard.edu/node/477

Perna, L. W. (2008). High school students' perceptions of local, national, and institutional scholarships. *Journal of Student Financial Aid, 37*(2), 4–16.

Perna, L.W. (2010). Toward a more complete understanding of the role of financial aid in promoting college enrollment: The importance of context. In J. C. Smart (Ed.), *Higher education: Handbook of theory and research* (pp. 129–179). Memphis, TN: Springer Science.

Pratt, R. H. (1892). *Official report of the Nineteenth Annual Conference of Charities and Correction.* Retrieved from http://quod.lib.umich.edu/n/ncosw/ACH8650.1892.001?rgn=main;view=fulltext

Redhouse, G. I. (2016). The university experiences of post-9/11 Native American veterans: Strategic support for inclusion, retention, and success. Unpublished doctoral dissertation, University of Arizona, Tucson, AZ.

Rockwell, S. J. (2010). *Indian affairs and the administrative state in the nineteenth century.* Cambridge, UK: Cambridge University Press.

Shone, C. (2010, October 22). For many on the Navajo Nation, it's been a long wait for power [Weblog post]. Retrieved from http://cronkitenewsonline.com/2010/10/for-many-navajos-its-been-a-long-wait-for-power/

Shotton, H. (2016, January 13). Educator Heather Shotton on Native American identity [Interview]. Retrieved from http://kgou.org/post/educator-heather-shotton-native-american-identity

Special Subcommittee on Indian Education. (1969). *Indian education: A national tragedy—A national challenge.* 1969 Report of the Committee on Public Labor and Welfare, U.S. Senate. Retrieved from http://files.eric.ed.gov/fulltext/ED034625.pdf

Stein, W. J. (2009). Tribal colleges and universities: Supporting the revitalization in Indian country. In L. S. Warner & G. E. Gipp (Eds.), *Tradition and culture in the millennium: Tribal colleges and universities* (pp. 17–34). Charlotte, NC: Information Age.

Tachine, A. (2015). Monsters and weapons: Navajo students' stories on their journeys toward college. Unpublished doctoral dissertation, University of Arizona, Tucson, AZ.

Tierney, W. G., Sallee, M. W., & Venegas, K. M. (2007, Fall). Access and financial aid: How American Indian students pay for college. *Journal of College Admissions, 197,* 14–23.

U.S. Census Bureau. (2011, November). *Profile American facts for features American Indian and Alaskan Native heritage month.* Retrieved from www.census.gov/newsroom/releases/archives/facts_for_features_special_editions/cb11-ff22.html

U.S. Executive Office of the President. (2014). *Native youth report.* Retrieved from www.whitehouse.gov/sites/default/files/docs/20141129nativeyouthreport_final.pdf

Wallenstein, P. (2008). *Higher education and the civil rights movement: White supremacy, black southerners, and college campuses.* Gainesville, FL: University Press of Florida.

West Virginia Secretary of State. (2017). *Business organization search.* Retrieved from http://apps.sos.wv.gov/business/corporations/searchadvanced.aspx

Willard, W. (1997). Outing, relocation, and employee assistance: The impact of federal Indian population dispersal programs in the Bay area. *Wicazo Sa Review, 12*(1), 29–46.

Wright, B. (1988). "For the children of infidels?": American Indian education in the colonial colleges. *American Indian Culture and Research Journal, 12*(3), 1–14.

NAKAY'S STORY

Nakay R. Flotte (Mescalero-Lipan Apache)

Shíí eí Nakay R. Flotte shíízhįį. Bíłł miik'a bołchi'yé shiideeshchįį. Shįį goosdezog ndé ch'ináķįį hałgaiyé nééssai. Ixé'hé bikégoindáan dóó ashóogi ndé'é ķọģįhéndé k'éh, nzhó dołéel. My name is Nakay Flotte, named by my parents as Roberto. I was born and raised in the Texas–Mexico borderlands. For at least seven generations, corn has been prepared the same way by women in this geographic region, from my great-great-great-great grandmother's time to *shíamá*, my grandmother, Lupe Natividad's time. I am original to *náada twid héndé*, tough desert peoples of the corn. My father's *k'eh* is also woven into the history of the borderlands desert. My paternal clan, the *ķọģįįhéndé* or sotol people, intermarried French mine owners of the region in the late 1800s, and the production of sotol (*ķọģįį*), a distilled spirit, became a family business for many generations. My family has lived around the Chihuahuan desert mountains on both sides of the border since before there was a United States or Mexico, and even before any European archive could trace, recall, or record our names and stories.

I come from a mixed-status family. I have undocumented siblings, cousins, aunts, and uncles. Many live as "undocumented" Indigenous peoples in their own bisected land. My parents were undocumented when I was young, so we worked and lived on the Mexican side in a small city called Ojinaga, Chihuahua. I attended school in Mexico until I was 15, when I had to leave my house because my family did not accept that I wanted to live as a gender-nonconforming person. I was a biologically born male unable to fit the gender roles ascribed to how "a man" should behave, dress, and act in society. I moved into my grandfather's decrepit 1940s mobile home and began high school in a border town with a population of fewer than 3,000.

I arrived to "the other side" of the border alone, naive, poor, and speaking not a word of English. I was publicly bullied and shamed every day in school for being a feminine boy. The boys and girls referred to me as *mariposa* (butterfly in Spanish) because I was one of three visibly identifiable queer people in my high school. I spent much of my time in the principal's office because I was often involved in some sort of physical conflict with students, teachers, and substitutes, usually due to their transphobia or homophobia. At first I opted to go home and delve into my depression, which led to intense thoughts and actions involving suicide. I was categorized as an "at-risk student" and was sent to speak to counselors, psychologists, and police officers. I noticed that these authorities, whether they were in the educational or public realm, often became invested in surveilling, questioning, and ripping off from my innate humanity. These were painful times. I opted to use meth to forget the cycle of distasteful events I experienced. To my school administration, I was yet another aggressive brown feminine Native boy in an education system aloof to the pain and suffering of Indigenous youth.

I refused to be a victim, much less their victim.

I then met other LGBT people in my high school who offered me unconditional support and love. They understood my anger and pain like nobody did before. Their openness to seeing me and each other beyond our "deviant" genders and sexualities allowed me to see that I was beautiful regardless of my parents' and others' opinions or morals. In two months, I was transferred from English as a second language to regular all-English courses, and I joined the basketball, cross-country, and track teams. Even among the school and home bullying—the ball, track, and field kept me focused and disciplined. Sports allowed me to foresee my life beyond aggression and to dream of a place where I could be fully accepted for my work ethic and perseverance. I forced my high school counselor to place me in all advanced placement and college credit courses, and I graduated at the top of my class. I was admitted to the top three public universities of Texas, and I accepted a full-ride offer to the University of Texas at Austin.

I was jovial and frightened the first time I crossed Austin's I-35 highway bridge in my small 2005 Chevy Colorado pickup truck. The city and culture outside of my homeland were intimidating. I had to learn new vocabulary as well as the social and institutional etiquette of the "Western world." My mind was bombarded by questions influenced by gender, class, race, and social etiquette: How should I approach a *madgani* stranger, who can I ask for help, how do I learn to study, and how do I handle everyday racism? In school I was often confused for a janitorial worker, I was paid less money for the same amount of work, and it was often assumed I was an undocumented student. When I responded that I was Native, Mescalero-Lipan Apache, many people saw me as a threat, and I was treated as a second-class citizen. People insisted I was not Native but "an illegal alien." My Native friends and I were often denied service in restaurants, and too often we experienced antagonistic interactions with intoxicated college students who mocked us by playing Indian, "acting gay," or calling us "wetbacks."

I joined and cofounded a number of queer, Native, and student sports clubs, which allowed me to become involved in a close-knit group of LGBT, Native, and Mexican students. We received support from the local Indigenous communities of the area, the Carrizo/Comecrudo Tribe of Texas and the Miakan Band of the Coahuiltecan Nation, and we were often invited to share sweat lodges and *hosh iztí or paxé* medicine ceremonies with them. Practicing our traditional Native religions was our mental health therapy. It encouraged many of us to be thankful for our opportunities and made us strong when facing the challenges of being low-income, Native, immigrant, and first-generation students. During my undergraduate career, I wrote an honor's thesis with the support of a Choctaw professor, one of only three female Native professors in the entire university. I was taught how to conduct research beneficial to the intellectual community as well as develop research projects that are valuable, accessible, and centered on the pragmatic needs of Indigenous peoples. I examined illegal mining activities on Indigenous sacred territory in southeastern Mexico, and I was named the 2012 Dean's Distinguished Graduate for the best thesis in the College of Liberal Arts. I graduated *summa cum laude*.

I took a year off after college and moved to Oakland, California, to pursue two unpaid internships, both in the nonprofit sector in the city of San Francisco. As a first-generation student, I did not have the social capital and understanding on how to find employment after college. Also, many professional employers did not hire me because I appeared androgynous. I worked cleaning yards, busing tables, offering tutoring services door to door, helping older people, and as a sex worker, just to afford rent and food. With the support and encouragement of a Xicano doctoral candidate attending Berkeley at that time, I opted to apply to graduate school. He edited my personal and project statements and guided me through the process. After eight months of living day to day in a small, shared studio apartment, I received the news that I was admitted into both the Harvard and Princeton anthropology PhD programs, as well as the medical anthropology program at Berkeley.

The journey to graduate school has been my most challenging and impactful career choice. I opted for the Harvard anthropology program because it offered the most freedom in developing unique and ethically conscious research projects. In a university where there are fewer than five Indigenous doctoral students and not one Native faculty, it becomes difficult to make sense of the direction and goals of your work. I was fortunate to find a space at the Harvard University Native American Program, where I was welcomed the first weeks of my graduate career. I have since forged relationships with the program's director, staff, and other students, and I am thankful I can share a space with other native students to talk, cope, and laugh at our everyday experiences with institutional erasure.

Graduate school is still a challenge. However, reflecting back, I have come to realize my successes have been supported by individuals and programs that accept my personal identity, understand the difficulties I have faced, and encourage my intellectual interests, which often don't fit the standard university mold. I am currently researching the long history of security collaborations and intelligence sharing between the United States and Mexico, a relationship created to detain and deport Central American refugees. In this research, I will explore Indigenous identities in the hopes of bringing a better understanding of our histories and our presence today.

5

JOURNEY INTO THE SCIENCES

Successful Native American STEM Programs

LeManuel Lee Bitsói (Diné) and Shelly C. Lowe (Diné)

> In sum, increasing success among racial and ethnic minority students in STEM is urgent for several reasons, including the fact that it is necessary for the economic well-being of individuals and the nation, America's competitiveness in the international marketplace, the moral and ethical obligation of educators to fight systemic inequities, and the need to adequately prepare STEM college graduates for the increasingly diverse and global STEM workforce. (Museus, Palmer, Davis, & Maramba, 2011, pp. 4–5)

Throughout our careers in higher education, we have been asked many times the following questions: Why aren't there more Native Americans pursuing science, technology, engineering, and math (STEM) degree programs or careers? Is it because Native Americans are anti-science? Is science part of your culture? As advocates for underrepresented minority students pursuing STEM[1] degrees, especially Native Americans, we turn these questions into teaching opportunities to begin conversations on how to increase the number of Indigenous scientists and researchers. Accordingly, this chapter begins with an introduction to Indigenous science perspective(s), followed by an overview of trends in STEM education attainment across the United States. We then highlight funding sources that support STEM-focused programs, particularly those that encompass community and institutional partnerships and the professional organizations focused on supporting Native students in STEM. Next, an introduction is provided to a few of the leading colleges and universities that graduate the highest number of Native American students in STEM programs, along with a review of tribal colleges and universities (TCUs) with successful and flourishing STEM programs. Last, recommendations to support the success of Native students in STEM will be provided.

Science and Culture

Whenever we have the opportunity to teach others about Native Americans and our desire for a pro-Indigenous approach to STEM education, we begin by simply stating that we have math and science deeply embedded within our cultures and traditional knowledge bases, just as other Indigenous people do worldwide. Our traditional way of knowing how to live with the land enabled us to develop sophisticated knowledge bases about animal husbandry, anatomy and physiology, botany and crop management, climate science, and astronomy, along with other forms of scientific knowledge. We have always understood what the terms *organic* and *range-free* mean. Moreover, we have ancestral knowledge about the power of nature in healing and living a well-balanced life through ethnobotany and ethnomedicine. Prior to Columbus's invasion, Native people were adding, subtracting, and multiplying numbers within a base-10 system. Tragically, during the assimilation years and the boarding school experience, we lost many of our languages, and our understanding of math was replaced with a system that did not communicate the base-10 meaning very well (Hankes, Whirlwind Soldier, & Davis, 1998).

As Native people, we rely on oral history to impart knowledge. Oral history has not always been considered a valid source of data. However, Brayboy (2005) challenges this notion through tribal critical race theory (TribalCrit) by asserting that oral history/information/stories are valid forms of data. Because oral history is often disregarded as legitimate knowledge, most people are not aware that STEM is not new to us; these subjects have been part of Indigenous cultures for centuries. Science is taught with ethnobotany through the use of plants for medicinal or artistic use. Biology is present in the agronomy and agricultural techniques of Native people, most notably in the practice of planting corn, beans, and squash next to each other. Technology can be found in the manner in which Native people use natural waterways to design and utilize irrigation canals for their farms. Engineering can be found in the architecture of homes and ceremonial structures—the portable teepee or traditional Navajo Hogan. Math can be found in the traditional counting systems of Indigenous people through pictures or knots on a counting rope. Anatomy and physiology are taught in the butchering of a deer, sheep, or buffalo. Astronomy and cosmology are also crucial to the way Native people tell the changing of the seasons and forecast weather.

Moreover, Indigenous technology existed over a millennium ago. Billy and Kuslikis (2009) point to the ceramic technology of the Anasazi culture as an illustration of such technology through their experimentation "with different combinations of clay, sand, and water: ceramic bowls, pots and dishes—indispensable tools of everyday life and a continuous source of innovation, as more specialized forms of ceramic were developed for specific social, ceremonial and trade uses" (p. 201). None of these ways of knowing were printed; thus, they were not considered by non-Natives to be science. Native people have always had STEM epistemologies in their worlds, but we use different words and concepts that are not always acknowledged by Western education. To Native people, these ways of knowing are part of life and continue to be passed on through oral traditions. Some colleges and universities, notably TCUs, have acknowledged this crucial link in the education of Native students, and this has resulted in efforts to broaden the participation of Native students in STEM fields.

Trends in STEM Education Attainment

A recent report from the U.S Department of Education (Chen & Soldner, 2013) summarizes the growing concerns over increasing student attrition in postsecondary STEM education. Snyder and Dillow (2011) report that STEM majors accounted for 14% of all enrolled undergraduates in 2007–2008, but Chen (2009) reports that 56% of these students left the field within 6 years of entering college and before graduating. A summary of studies on STEM majors shows that underrepresented minorities along with women, low-income students, and first-generation students tend to leave STEM fields of study at higher rates (Chen & Soldner, 2013). Numerous studies have shown that underrepresented students are as likely to enter STEM majors but are less likely to earn a degree in a STEM field (Tsui, 2007). As early as freshman year, students from lower socioeconomic status backgrounds with weaker academic preparation are confronted with negative experiences in introductory math[2] and science courses, leading to lower grades and often a change in major. In addition, due to their backgrounds and experiences in college science and math courses, these groups tend to exhibit lower self-efficacy, leading to less motivation and confidence in their ability to succeed in the field (Chen & Soldner, 2013; Tsui, 2007).

Both Tsui (2007) and the U.S. Department of Education (Chen & Soldner, 2013) point out other factors influencing STEM attrition in higher education. Lack of quality academic advising and career counseling is particularly damaging to students in STEM fields, along with poor teaching and a lack of engagement from supportive faculty both inside and outside the classroom through hands-on research. A lack of mentors and professionals with similar backgrounds also contributed to a lack of persistence in STEM fields, along with a feeling of isolation due to few classmates and peers from similar backgrounds in their major. Limited institutional support, in the form of academic support such as tutoring, to financial support through scholarships and grant aid, also contributes to high attrition. Last, not having a clear understanding of how science professions contribute to society also influenced students to transfer out of STEM fields into major fields perceived to be more beneficial to communities and society overall.

Tsui's (2007) review of effective strategies to increase diversity in STEM fields identified multiple intervention avenues to support underrepresented STEM majors. Overnight residential summer bridge programs were found to be positively related to successful retention in engineering. Frequent, naturally formed mentoring relationships with faculty or staff as well as a strong social support network were key to the academic persistence of STEM majors, but the ability of faculty members to provide positive and effective mentoring was essential. Engaging hands-on research, on or off campus, particularly with faculty or in the professional industry, increased the number of students pursuing STEM degrees and careers. In addition, both summer research programs and conducting research with faculty helped to solidify students' career choice and self-efficacy. Formalized tutoring, academic workshops and seminars, and intrusive advising, given frequently, led to fewer students withdrawing from STEM courses and switching to non-STEM majors. Although not an academic intervention, financial stability in college was found to be positively related to entering and completing STEM degrees, but working 15 hours or more to maintain financial stability increased noncompletion of the degree.

Although much of the literature related to STEM education attainment is focused on the broader population of underrepresented students and not specifically on Native students, much may be gleaned for how Native students can be supported in STEM education. In the next section, we explore national organizations that provide direct support for increasing Native student presence and success in STEM education and professions. These organizations may provide fiscal support, such as federal agencies and nonprofit foundation, or they may be nonprofit organizations that directly support professionalization in the field.

National Support for Natives in STEM

Federal training grants focused on STEM are available for postsecondary institutions, including TCUs. To that end, the following federal agencies have supported notable programs focused on recruiting, retaining, and increasing the number of Native Americans at the undergraduate, postbaccalaureate, doctoral, and postdoctoral levels. The National Institutes of Health[3] (NIH), in collaboration with the Indian Health Service (IHS), provides funding for the Native American Research Centers for Health (NARCH) program. According to the NARCH website,

> The NARCH initiative supports partnerships between American Indian/ Alaska Native (AI/AN) tribes or tribally-based organizations and institutions that conduct intensive academic-level biomedical research. NARCH provides opportunities for conducting research, research training and faculty development to meet the needs of AI/AN communities. As a developmental process, tribes and tribal organizations are able to build a research infrastructure, including a core component for capacity building and the possibility of reducing the many health disparities so prevalent in AI/AN communities. (National Institute of General Medical Sciences, n.d.-b)

With this program, awards are made to the tribal entity that then subcontracts with partnering research programs in colleges and universities or medical institutions. Tribes take the lead in identifying their health priorities, research and training needs, educational level for participation (K–12 through postdoctoral degree), and institutional partnerships. Although the program is focused on reducing health disparities, many NARCH grantees have developed programs to increase overall STEM participation through higher education degree attainment, hands-on research, and professional training opportunities.

In addition to the NARCH program, the NIH also supports the Research Initiative for Scientific Enhancement (RISE) Program and the Institutional Research and Academic Career Development Award (IRACDA). The RISE Program is "a developmental program that seeks to increase the capacity of students underrepresented in the biomedical sciences to complete PhD degrees in these fields. The program provides grants to institutions with a commitment and history of developing students from populations underrepresented in biomedical sciences" (National Institute of General Medical Sciences, n.d.-c). With a purpose similar to RISE, IRACDA funds partnerships and consortia "between research-intensive institutions and partner institutions that have a historical mission and a demonstrated commitment to providing training, encouragement and assistance to students from groups underrepresented in the biomedical research enterprise of the nation" (National Institute of General Medical Sciences, n.d.-a). IRACDA provides traditional post-doc research opportunities with mentored teaching opportunities at the partner institution to increase the diversity of faculty in biomedical fields.

The National Science Foundation (NSF) has also made inroads in reaching out directly to TCUs through the TCU Program (TCUP). To provide a skilled labor force so Native Americans can serve their own communities in scientific and technical endeavors, TCUP funding

> provides awards to Tribal Colleges and Universities, Alaska Native-serving institutions, and Native Hawaiian-serving institutions to promote high quality science (including sociology, psychology, anthropology, economics, statistics, and other social and behavioral science as well as natural science and education disciplines), technology, engineering and mathematics (STEM) education, research, and outreach. (National Science Foundation, n.d.-b)

The first TCUP awards were made in September 2001. The program's inaugural projects broadly address institutional needs at a variety of institutions, including the evaluation of existing STEM curricula, professional development for faculty and staff, hands-on learning and research experiences for students, improved academic and professional support for students, increased connections with tribal members and community resources, and improvements to facilities (National Science Foundation, 2002).

Through funding from federal agencies such as NIH and NSF, higher education institutions have developed and strengthened programs to increase enrollment and degree attainment by Native students in STEM fields. Support for Native students in STEM also comes from nonfederal entities such as the Alfred P. Sloan Foundation, the home of the Sloan Indigenous Graduate Partnership, whose goal is "to strengthen and expand university initiatives to recruit, train, and graduate American Indian and Alaska Native students in STEM graduate programs" (Alfred P. Sloan Foundation, n.d.). Institutional partners in this program include both campuses of the University of Alaska (Anchorage and Fairbanks), the University of Arizona, the public universities of Montana (Montana State University, Montana Tech, and University of Montana), and Purdue University. Each university is charged with recruiting and admitting a certain number of Native American students into both master's and doctoral STEM degree programs. Each institution must also commit to providing financial assistance and mentoring support to participating students. The Sloan Foundation provides additional funding to students and offers professional development opportunities.

Students in many of these programs receive additional professionalization support through national organizations such as the American Indian Science and Engineering Society (AISES), the Society for the Advancement of Chicanos/Hispanics & Native Americans in Science (SACNAS), and the Association of American Indian Physicians (AAIP). Founded in 1977, AISES is a collective of more than 4,000 individual members, 189 college-level student chapters, 15 professional chapters, and 158 K–12-affiliated schools that support the organization's goal of substantially increasing the representation of North America's Indigenous peoples in STEM studies and careers. AISES "Awareness and Retention" programs begin at the precollege level with virtual science fairs, an energy-specific science fair, workshops to support student participation in science fairs, a science bowl, and paid internships. College-level programs for "Access and Success" also include virtual science fair participation and internships but also include the Lighting the Pathway program to support students interested in entering faculty careers, providing engineering doctoral students with financial assistance to attend the national conference, and a program to support partnerships between tribal colleges and mainstream institutions to increase student access to energy research and education. Professional-level programs support "Leadership and Change" by awarding notable science professionals, providing financial assistance to post docs and early career faculty to attend the national conference, connecting new professionals to mentors, and maintaining a job board. The AISES student leadership summit offers an opportunity for college students to connect with professionals, and events at both the national and regional conferences are offered for all participant levels (American Indian Science and Engineering Society, n.d.).

Recognizing the need to diversify the nation's scientific workforce, a group of Chicano and Native American scientists created SACNAS in 1973. The organization continues to support the success of its members, beginning in college through their professional careers, to increase quality research for use by communities, influence policies to reduce barriers in STEM education, and provide guidance to better represent all cultures and ethnicities in science (Society for the Advancement of Chicanos/Hispanics & Native Americans in Science, n.d.-b). Specific support for Native American students is provided through Scholars in Science: Native American Path (SSNAP). SSNAP provides year-round mentoring, workshops, and networking for undergraduate- and graduate-level Native students in STEM degree programs. To achieve optimal support for Native students, SACNAS partners with AIHEC, AISES, IHS, and NARCH grantees (Society for the Advancement of Chicanos/Hispanics & Native Americans in Science, n.d.-a).

Prior to the creation of SACNAS and the founding of AISES, 14 American Indian and Alaska Native physicians came together to create an organization to improve the health of American Indian and Alaska Natives by supporting and providing services to their communities. Established in 1971, the AAIP sought to encourage Native students to enter and persist in health-related degree programs. Beyond providing support and encouragement to students with programming similar to AISES and SACNAS, AAIP also sought avenues to honor and include traditional healing practices. Forums where modern and traditional medicine can be combined are held by the AAIP in an effort to enhance healthcare delivery to American Indian/Alaska Native populations. A yearly conference is held for all members, and an intensive weeklong summer program is offered to high school juniors and seniors interested in entering health careers (Association of American Indian Physicians, n.d.).

Although there is much national support for Native student access to STEM fields, institutional support remains a key component of student success. Organizations such as AISES, SACNAS, and AAIP are able to provide culturally based mentoring, internship opportunities, and financial assistance for professional development, but higher education institutions, many with the support of federal and organizational funding, continue to provide the educational preparation for STEM careers. The next section looks at some of the leading colleges and universities that are supporting and graduating Native American students in STEM degree programs.

Top Mainstream Academic Institutions for Native American STEM Graduates

We begin by reviewing the list of leading colleges and universities that graduate the highest number of Native American students in STEM programs at the bachelor's level. In Table 5.1, we see that institutions range from liberal arts colleges to research-focused non-Native college and universities (NNCUs) throughout the country, including one TCU, Haskell Indian Nations University (National Science Foundation, 2017a). It is important to note that states with high Native populations tend to have institutions awarding higher numbers of STEM degrees to Native students.[4] Multiple institutions in Oklahoma, Arizona, California, and New Mexico rank among the top institutions awarding STEM degrees at all levels to Native students. Fort Lewis College, the only Colorado institution ranked in the top 20, is in proximity to multiple tribal groups in Arizona, New Mexico, Utah, and Colorado but, more uniquely, offers a full tuition waiver for all enrolled Native students. Although the University of Phoenix is listed as one of the leading institutions awarding STEM degrees to Native American students, our examination of individual institutions is limited to the traditional brick-and-mortar institutions because it is unclear how Native American students are recruited and supported through online institutions.[5]

In the state of Oklahoma, multiple institutions provide Indigenous-focused programming and support in STEM fields. At Oklahoma State University (OSU), these programs are offered in the Center for Health Sciences (CHS) by the Office for the Advancement of American Indians in Medicine and Science (OAAIMS). Launched in 2014, OAAIMS's goals are to increase the enrollment and retention of Native students in health-related programs

TABLE 5.1

Top 20 Academic Institutions Awarding STEM Bachelor's Degrees to American Indian and Alaska Native Graduates, 2011–2014

Top 20 Institutions	3,663
Oklahoma State University, Stillwater	294
University of Oklahoma, Norman	289
Northeastern State University	283
University of New Mexico, Albuquerque	244
Arizona State University, Tempe	231
Fort Lewis College	225
University of North Carolina–Pembroke	218
Northern Arizona University	206
University of Washington, Seattle	199
University of Phoenix, Online	187
East Central University	157
University of Arizona	155
Haskell Indian Nations University	151
Portland State University	136
Southeastern Oklahoma State University	136
California State University, Long Beach	130
Ashford University	123
University of California, Davis	108
Dartmouth College	103
New Mexico State University	88
Other Institutions	9,831

at CHS while building relationships with Oklahoma tribes to address their health and wellness needs (Oklahoma State University Center for Health Sciences, n.d.-a). OAAIMS became an institutional partner and host for two programs designed and coordinated by Native Explorers, a nonprofit organization based in Oklahoma City, Oklahoma. Native Explorers, created by the Chickasaw and Cherokee Nations, provides educational programs for both K–12 Native students and current Native college students (Native Explorers, n.d.). The Native Explorers programs at OSU-CHS are designed around the disciplines of anatomy and vertebrate paleontology and provide an array of hands-on, off-campus activities to introduce participants to science exploration, the scientific method, as well as the traditional cultural importance of natural resource management and historic site preservation (Oklahoma State University Center for Health Sciences, n.d.-b).

An additional program offered by OAAIMS is the Native OKstar summer intensive research program. Native OKstar participants are high school juniors and seniors assigned to work with a Native faculty member at CHS on an eight-week summer research project. In addition to hands-on research in the medical field, participants are matched with current Native medical students entering their second year of medical school. The program intends to introduce the realities of medical school and encourage participants to enter health-related degree programs (Oklahoma State University Center for Health Sciences, n.d.-b). Once Native students enter as new freshmen or transfer students at OSU, the Native American Resiliency through Education and Leadership Program provides support to promote a successful transition into the university community through mentorship, Native leadership, and access to a strong Native community both on and off campus (Oklahoma State University Native American Student Association, n.d.).

At the University of Oklahoma (OU), the Department of Chemistry and Biochemistry provides two summer K–12 outreach programs that incorporate Indigenous cultural knowledge and heritage into chemistry lectures. In these programs, "Oklahoma high school students engage in the extraction of chemicals from the Echinacea purpurea plants," which are indigenous to Oklahoma and traditionally used by many tribes in the state. Curricula in the STEM-to-Store Academy and Sooner Upward Bound programs focus on introducing students to the chemistry and history of natural and herbal medicines, connecting students to the study of chemistry, botany, mathematics, medicine, history, and Native American studies (University of Oklahoma Department of Chemistry and Biochemistry, n.d.). Additionally, through a partnership with the College of Engineering, Price College of Business, and the Native American Studies Department, OU offers an American Indian STEM and Business Day for Native high school students in Oklahoma. This event serves as an opportunity to introduce Native students to potential majors in STEM and Business through presentations and interaction with faculty, staff, and current Native students at the university (Watts, 2015).

At the University of New Mexico (UNM), the Engineering Student Services office provides specific support services to Native American students majoring in STEM degree programs. To assist in the matriculation and success of students, the Native Americans in Science, Technology, Engineering and Mathematics program provides academic support, informational workshops, a supportive community, academic scholarships, professional conference travel funds, internships, and employment opportunities. To participate in the program, students must be active members of UNM's AISES chapter or other Native American-focused student organizations (University of New Mexico, n.d.). UNM's Health Sciences Center houses 2 programs to support Native students in the health sciences. Both programs, the Center for Native American Health and the Institute for Indigenous Knowledge and Development, focus their work on connecting students to the specific needs of tribal communities, particularly in New Mexico. Students are introduced to training in cultural humility, able to hear directly from tribal leaders through the Tribal Leaders' Public Health Symposium, and introduced to community-based participatory research with a focus on respecting the tribal sovereignty of New Mexico's 23 tribes and their right to lead healthcare decisions by relying on local and unique knowledge, core cultural value systems, and traditional health beliefs (University of New Mexico Health Sciences Center, n.d.).

Haskell Indian Nations University (Haskell), the only TCU to be ranked among the top 20 institutions awarding bachelor's degrees in STEM to Native students, offers multiple avenues of support along with culturally specific programs to encourage degree attainment in STEM fields. "The College of Natural and Social Sciences supports Indigenous-centered teaching and learning initiatives to advance systems of life-enhancement for all peoples and places on our Mother Earth" (Haskell Indian Nations University, n.d.-a). The National Aeronautics and Space Administration (NASA) Experiential Learning Opportunity (TCU-ELO) at Haskell assists tribes in preparing for climate change by directly addressing the lack of infrastructure and resources in tribal communities. NASA resources are focused on providing climate change education and training in geospatial technology through TCU infrastructure development and summer research opportunities and externships for students (Haskell Indian Nations University, n.d.-c). The Haskell Environmental Research Studies also focuses on the effects of climate change on Indigenous communities by involving faculty in research on key hazardous substance problems on tribal lands and the dissemination of information to tribal communities (Haskell Environmental Research Studies, n.d.). To ensure student success in STEM degree programs, Haskell also offers a math program with the mission "to provide all students with an understanding of mathematics appropriate to their discipline" (Haskell Indian Nations University, n.d.-b) by providing a wide range of math course options, beginning with a basic introduction to algebra and algebra concepts to courses in Linear Algebra, Differential Equations, Calculus III, and High Power Rocketry. Haskell also provides avenues for students interested in biomedical sciences to successfully transition from the institution to other 4-year universities through the 500 Nations Bridge Collaboration funded by the NIH (University of Kansas, n.d.).

Haskell and these notable NNCUs are all committed to recruiting, retaining, and graduating Native American students in STEM fields, as evidenced by their commitment to student success programs. These programs range from multicultural STEM offices to sophisticated health partnerships with tribal communities and organizations. Their academic offerings also take into account Indigenous scientific epistemologies, and they are recognized and respected by Native and non-Native faculty. Through institutionalized support, complemented by federal funding, these institutions have the luxury of offering robust student support programming with rigorous research internships throughout the country. Collectively, these institutions have created welcoming and supportive environments for Native American students to thrive and persist to graduation in a STEM discipline.

Top TCUs for Native American STEM Graduates

Our next review is of the leading TCUs that graduate the highest number of Native American students in STEM programs at the associate degree level. Of the top 20 institutions on this list,[6] 7 are TCUs (Diné College, Oglala Lakota College, Navajo Technical University, Salish Kootenai College, Haskell Indian Nations University, Little Big Horn College, and Sitting Bull College). Again, it is important to note that institutions located within states with high Native populations and those closest to large tribal communities have higher numbers of associate degrees awarded to Native students. Except for Haskell, each of the TCUs on the list is located on or within tribal reservations and territories.

Tribal self- determination is crucial to nation building for tribal nations, and the Navajo nation was the first tribe to establish a TCU—Navajo Community College, now known as Diné College. The Navajo nation is where we begin our analysis. "In creating an institution of higher education, the Navajo Nation sought to encourage Navajo youth to become contributing members of the Navajo Nation and the world society. The College serves residents of the 26,000 square-mile Navajo Nation, which spans the states of Arizona, New Mexico, and Utah" (Diné College, n.d.-c). In addition to Diné College, the nation also operates Navajo Technical University (NTU), formerly known as the Crownpoint Institute of Technology.

Diné College offers six associate of science degrees (biology, general science, health occupation, environmental science, agroecology, and public health) that prepare students to transfer to a four-year program or vocational training. In addition, a bachelor of science in biology and a bachelor of science in secondary education with a science track and a mathematics track are offered. The degree in biology provides enhanced knowledge and appreciation of life on earth while also providing courses and training that will enable students to succeed in academics, develop a career path, pursue graduate studies, obtain employment and promotion in the workforce, and serve the Navajo nation. The bachelor of science in secondary education prepares students to be certified to teach high school biology or other high school science and math courses, particularly on the Navajo reservation, where these teachers are in high demand (Diné College, n.d.-a). Through a TCUP grant, the Diné College STEM program provides programs, services, and instruction focused on place- and inquiry-based approaches and internships. A three-day STEM camp is offered in the Chuska Mountains to introduce middle- and high school students to introductory STEM concepts in math, engineering, and scientific research techniques. The Diné Environmental Institute highlights research-based learning to provide a progressive system of student learning that aims to develop determination and self-reliance in each STEM student (Diné College, n.d.-b). Each of these programs is focused on addressing the needs of the Navajo people and allows students to see directly how careers in STEM fields contribute to their community.

NTU offers associate of science, associate of applied science, bachelor of science, and bachelor of applied science degrees (Navajo Technical University, n.d.-b). For early outreach into STEM degrees, NTU offers several weeklong summer programs for kindergarten- through high school–age students. One of the camps is focused on learning math through music and offers students classes on Navajo sheepherding songs and classical opera, with concerts held in the NTU Hogan by local artists and teachers from Julliard (Navajo Technical University, n.d.-a). In partnership with NASA, the university offers middle-school students guided visits to local cultural and geological sites. Led by scientists and traditional medicine people, day trips to these sites introduce scientific knowledge from both a Diné way of knowing and a Western scientific way of knowing (Navajo Technical University, n.d.-c). The newest summer camp offers middle- and high school students an opportunity to explore technologies such as three-dimensional printing and modeling. An effort to develop the next generation of engineers, artists, and inventors, the Navajo Maker Summer Camp introduces participants to computer software to create three-dimensional race cars and smart phone accessories (Navajo Technical University, n.d.-d). Both Diné College and Navajo Technical University operate satellite campuses across the Navajo reservation and are grounded in the Diné traditional education principles.[7]

Another TCU ranked high among the top 20 institutions awarding associate degrees in science and engineering is Oglala Lakota College (OLC) in South Dakota. OLC is a regional leader in environmental science, offering bachelor of science degrees in Natural Resources and Natural Science with an emphasis in the areas of Conservation Biology and Earth Science. OLC also offers associate degree programs in Life Sciences and Natural Resources.

Students who complete degrees in the natural sciences at OLC are required to take courses that incorporate traditional Lakota concepts concerning language, land, plants, and animals. In addition, "The Math, Science, and Technology learning philosophy emphasizes a constructivist framework, a hands-on approach to improve the quality of life on the Reservation through science and technology" (Oglala Lakota College, n.d.). With degree programs focused on natural resource management, OLC intends to provide its members with an education for future career or graduate school opportunities, as well as provide the tribe with expertly trained employees capable of properly caring for the Pine Ridge Reservation.

To engage students prior to entering college, OLC participates in the South Dakota Jump Start Program (Jump Start) (South Dakota Board of Regents, n.d.). Through this program, potential college-bound students in South Dakota are matched with advisers who work one on one with them to assess whether they are ready for college, what kind of college they might want to explore if they are ready, and the necessary steps required to apply and prepare for college attendance. Access advisers work with students in their high schools and even in their homes, bringing family members into the college-going conversation. When students choose to explore college going, they are given step-by-step advice and support, such as registering to take the ACT, visiting college campuses, filling out applications for financial aid, and completing the college admissions application. The Jump Start program works to ensure that obstacles faced by students when they are just beginning to consider college are identified and addressed in a timely manner. Once the student has enrolled in college, a Jump Start adviser is available on campus to continue supporting the student's first year. Eight South Dakota public institutions participate in the program, with OLC as the only tribal college participant.

Unlike the majority institutions that were analyzed in the previous section, the inextricable link among Native language, culture, and traditions within STEM programs at TCUs is clear. The focus on life sciences, environmental sciences, and information technology (and other STEM-related fields) through place- and inquiry-based approaches, philosophies that emphasize a constructivist framework, hands-on approaches to improve the quality of life on reservations through science and technology, notably supports the advancement of tribal members as they seek to become self-reliant and self-determined members of society. Despite not having rich coffers for extensive academic programs and readily available cutting-edge technology, TCUs are offering STEM degrees at the associate and bachelor levels with ambitious plans to offer degrees at the graduate level (Holdman, 2016). With affordable tuition and modest student activity fees, TCUs offer robust student enrichment and support programming (including mentoring), along with affiliations in AISES and SACNAS. This situation bodes well for TCU students because it allows them to engage in professional development activities outside their campus. Collectively, TCUs provide dynamic STEM academic offerings to students, campus educators, and community members, which contribute to nation building on many levels while remaining true to their commitment to maintain language and culture in the twenty-first century.

Recruiting, Retaining, and Graduating Native American Students in STEM

Based on this review of the leading higher education institutions that graduate the highest number of Native American students in STEM programs, a number of themes have emerged to ensure that Native American students persist and graduate with a STEM degree. The most common themes that emerged include recognizing and valuing Indigenous scientific knowledge and incorporating such knowledge into curricula, outreach and engagement through research and internship opportunities, the importance of early outreach, and the impact of national funding and organizations. Each of the institutions reviewed has Native and non-Native faculty who understand and know how to work with Native students to ensure their success through teaching, mentoring, and collaborative research opportunities. In addition, the academic offerings and curriculum take into account or directly include Indigenous scientific epistemologies. The STEM degree programs in these institutions also provide links among Native language, culture, and traditions through place- and inquiry-based approaches that directly address the math, science, and engineering needs of the tribal communities served.

In some capacity, each institution has a program or office that provides students (and faculty) opportunities to connect with tribal communities through community-based research projects or internships. Collectively, these efforts honor tribal sovereignty by addressing the real day-to-day needs and concerns of tribes stemming from environmental realities such as climate change, water resource management and protection, cultural site preservation, and a number of other concerns requiring skilled STEM employees. Hands-on research with tribal communities allows students to connect the material being studied to real-life problems and career opportunities. In many instances, tribal leaders are brought in to discuss and identify areas of high concern that can be addressed by institutional curriculum and student research. Outreach is not limited to current students, however.

A number of the institutions reviewed provide early outreach to STEM careers via weeklong or intensive summer programs for youth starting as early as kindergarten. Programs with hands-on projects, particularly focused on cultural resources and management or introductions to math and technology, allow young students to start thinking about STEM as a possible career opportunity. Programs offered on-site at an institution with overnight stays introduce these students to college life and help them to explore college going early on. Providing individuals who can support the exploration of college going with a STEM focus is key to helping these students understand the challenges of college going and how to prepare for the rigorous curriculum in STEM degree programs. Continued advising and mentoring from academic faculty and support staff throughout the college career is also key to providing the encouragement needed to persist to graduation.

Although mentoring and advising are available on campus, it is also important for Native students to extend themselves beyond their campus comfort zones. Extramural professional development is accomplished through multicultural and multidisciplinary venues such as AISES and SAC-NAS, which provide much-needed career mentoring and professional networking. Supporting AISES and SACNAS chapters on campus also provide students an avenue for informal peer mentoring and connection. Each of the institutions reviewed has an active AISES and/or SACNAS chapter. Although these institutions were not part of the Sloan Indigenous Graduate Partnership, it is clear that financial support for Native students in STEM programs is needed. Financial support through scholarships and fellowships is key. In addition, financial support for STEM access programs, such as funding from NIH and the NARCH grants, has played a major role in increasing Native student participation in STEM.

Although many more Native American–serving institutions (including TCUs) could have been included in this chapter, not all institutions have information that is readily available and accessible. It was important to highlight these colleges and universities to illustrate the investments they are making to ensure that Native American students are entering, persisting, and graduating with degrees in a STEM discipline. Furthermore, this analysis provides scaffolding for future research endeavors that can be even more in depth and comprehensive.

Notes

1. In this chapter, STEM includes areas of study, academic majors, and academic degree and certificate programs in biological/agricultural sciences, computer sciences, engineering, mathematics, and physical sciences (National Science Board, 2016).

2. College math courses in particular present challenges to Native students' decision to enter STEM majors but also to even consider college. Defined as the

"choke point" by a TCU faculty member (Conrad & Gasman, 2015), this issue has also led to a national calculus reform movement (Tsui, 2007).

    3. The National Institutes of Health is made up of 27 institutes and centers. See www.nih.gov/about-nih/who-we-are/organization.

    4. Go to www.nsf.gov/statistics/2017/nsf17310/data.cfm for more information on the top institutions awarding S&E degrees to American Indians and Alaska Natives.

    5. The University of Phoenix is not a brick-and-mortar institution, so it is difficult to ascertain whether there are student organizations for Native American students.

    6. See https://www.nsf.gov/statistics/2017/nsf17310/static/data/tab4-5.pdf

    7. Both Diné College and Navajo Technical University operate under the traditional Navajo principle of Sa'ah Naaghái Bik'eh Hozhoo. See http://w.dinecollege.edu/about/philosophy.php.

References

Alfred P. Sloan Foundation. (n.d.). *Sloan Indigenous Graduate Partnership*. Retrieved from https://sloan.org/programs/higher-education/education-underrepresented-groups/sloan-indigenous-graduate-partnership

American Indian Science and Engineering Society. (n.d.). *About AISES*. Retrieved from http://www.aises.org/about/

Association of American Indian Physicians. (n.d.). *Association of American Indian Physicians*. Retrieved from www.aaip.org/

Billy, C. L., & Kuslikis, A. (2009). Technology at the TCUs. In L. S. Warner & G. E. Gipp (Eds.), *Tradition and culture in the millennium: Tribal colleges and universities. Educational policy in the 21st century: Opportunities, challenges and solutions* (pp. 201–208). Charlotte, NC: Information Age.

Brayboy, B. J. M. (2005). Toward a tribal critical race theory in education. *The Urban Review, 37*(5), 425–446.

Chen, X. (2009). *Students who study science, technology, engineering, and mathematics (STEM) in postsecondary education* (NCES 2009-161). Washington DC: National Center for Education Statistics, Institute of Education Sciences, U.S. Department of Education.

Chen, X., & Soldner, M. (2013). *STEM attrition: College students' paths into and out of STEM fields* (NCES 2014-001). Washington DC: National Center for Education Statistics, Institute of Education Sciences, U.S. Department of Education.

Conrad, C., & Gasman, M. (2015). Tribal colleges and universities: Culturally responsive places. In *Educating a diverse nation: Lessons from minority-serving institutions* (pp. 35–92). Cambridge, MA: Harvard University Press.

Diné College. (n.d.-a) *Academic degrees and certificates*. Retrieved from www.dinecollege.edu/academics/academic.php

Diné College. (n.d.-b). *Diné Environmental Institute*. Retrieved from www.dinecollege.edu/institutes/dei.php

Diné College. (n.d.-c). *History*. Retrieved from www.dinecollege.edu/about/history.php

Gipp, D. M. (2009). The story of AIHEC in tradition and culture. In L. S. Warner & G. E. Gipp (Eds.), *Tradition and culture in the millennium: Tribal colleges and universities* (pp. 7–16). Charlotte, NC: Information Age.

Guillory, J. P., & Ward, K. (2008). Tribal colleges and universities: Identity, invisibility, and current issues. In M. B. Gasman, B. Baez, & C. S. V. Turner (Eds.), *Understanding minority-serving institutions* (pp. 91–110). Albany, NY: SUNY Press.

Hankes, J. T., Whirlwind Soldier, L., & Davis, A. (1998). Investigating the advantages of constructing multidigit numeration understanding through Oneida and Lakota Native languages. *Journal of American Indian Education, 38*(1), 15–35.

Haskell Environmental Research Studies. (n.d.). *Who we are*. Retrieved from www.hersinstitute.org/#!/page_about

Haskell Indian Nations University. (n.d.-a). *College of Natural and Social Sciences*. Retrieved from www.haskell.edu/academics/college-of-natural-and-social-sciences/

Haskell Indian Nations University. (n.d.-b). *Department of Mathematics*. Retrieved from www.haskell.edu/academics/math/

Haskell Indian Nations University. (n.d.-c). *Haskell NASA Experiential Learning Opportunity (TCU-ELO) program*. Retrieved from www.haskell.edu/sponsored-programs/nasa-elo-program/

Holdman, J. (2016, December 11). Master's programs growing at tribal colleges. *The Bismark Tribune*. Retrieved from http://bismarcktribune.com/news/state-and-regional/master-s-programs-growing-at-tribal-colleges/article_56d53c4b-1d4e-56c5-9930-9494f7b3d1db.html

Museus, S. D., Palmer, R. T., Davis, R. J., & Maramba, D. C. (2011). Racial and ethnic minority students' success in STEM education. *ASHE Higher Education Report, 36*(6).

National Institute of General Medical Sciences. (n.d.-a). *Institutional Research and Academic Career Development Awards (IRACDA) K12*. Retrieved from www.nigms.nih.gov/Training/CareerDev/Pages/TWDInstRes.aspx

National Institute of General Medical Sciences. (n.d.-b). *Native American Research Centers for Health (NARCH)*. Retrieved from www.nigms.nih.gov/Research/CRCB/NARCH/Pages/default.aspx

National Institute of General Medical Sciences (n.d.-c). *Research Initiative for Scientific Enhancement (RISE) Program (R25)*. Retrieved from www.nigms.nih.gov/Training/RISE/Pages/default.aspx

National Science Board. (2016). *Science and Engineering Indicators 2016*. National Science Foundation, Arlington, VA. Retrieved from https://www.nsf.gov/statistics/2016/nsb20161/#/report

National Science Foundation. (2002). *NSF's tribal colleges and universities program: Nations united in improving science and technology education for Native Americans, NSF 02-072*. Retrieved from www.nsf.gov/pubs/2002/nsf02072/nsf02072.pdf

National Science Foundation. (2017a). TABLE 5-12. Top 20 academic institutions awarding S&E bachelor's degrees, by race or ethnicity of minority graduates: 2011–2014. Retrieved from www.nsf.gov/statistics/2017/nsf17310/static/data/tab5-12.pdf

National Science Foundation. (2017b). TABLE 4-5. Top 20 academic institutions awarding associates degrees in S&E, S&E technologies, and interdisciplinary or other science fields, by race or ethnicity of minority graduates: 2011–2014. Retrieved from www.nsf.gov/statistics/2017/nsf17310/static/data/tab4-5.pdf

National Science Foundation. (n.d.). *Tribal colleges and universities program (TCUP).* Retrieved from www.nsf.gov/funding/pgm_summ.jsp?pims_id=5483

Native Explorers. (n.d.). *2017 Program overview Native explorers.* Retrieved from www.nativeexplorers.org/Websites/NativeExplorerslive/images/2017%20 Native%20Explorers%20FlyerDistrib.pdf

Navajo Technical University. (n.d.-a). *The Heartbeat Project at NTU–Math to music.* Retrieved from http://www.navajotech.edu/campus-life/upcoming-events/991-the-heartbeat-project-at-ntu-math-to-music

Navajo Technical University. (n.d.-b). *History; degrees; STEM lab; Navajo Technical University.* Retrieved from www.navajotech.edu

Navajo Technical University. (n.d.-c). *NASA/Navajo summer camp.* Retrieved from www .navajotech.edu/campus-life/upcoming-events/988-nasa-navajo-summer-camp

Navajo Technical University. (n.d.-d). *Youth camp promotes science, innovation, and making at Navajo Technical University.* Retrieved from www.navajotech.edu/ campus-life/announcements/news-releases/987-youth-camp-promotes-science-innovation-and-making-at-navajo-technical-university

Oglala Lakota College. (n.d.). *Math, science, & technology.* Retrieved from www.olc .edu/departments/math_sci_tech.htm

Oklahoma State University Center for Health Sciences. (n.d.-a). *OAAIMS mission, vision and goals.* Retrieved from www.healthsciences.okstate.edu/oaaims/mission.php

Oklahoma State University Center for Health Sciences. (n.d.-b). *OAAIMS programs.* Retrieved from www.healthsciences.okstate.edu/oaaims/programs.php

Oklahoma State University Native American Student Association. (n.d.). *Native American resiliency through education and leadership program.* Retrieved from http://orgs.okstate.edu/nasa/NARELP.html

Snyder, T. D., & Dillow, S. A. (2011). *Digest of Education Statistics, 2010* (NCES 2011-015). Washington DC: National Center for Education Statistics, Institute of Education Sciences, U.S. Department of Education.

Society for the Advancement of Chicanos/Hispanics and Native Americans in Science. (2015). *Our history, society for advancement of Hispanics/Chicanos and Native Americans in science.* Retrieved from http://sacnas.org/about/our-history

Society for the Advancement of Chicanos/Hispanics and Native Americans in Science. (n.d.-a). *Native American programs.* Retrieved from http://sacnas.org/what-we-do/ native-american-programs/

Society for the Advancement of Chicanos/Hispanics and Native Americans in Science (n.d.-b). *SACNAS brief history and overview.* Retrieved from http://bio.sacnas.org/ uploads/Marketing/SACNAS_History.pdf

South Dakota Board of Regents. (n.d.). *South Dakota Jump Start.* Retrieved from www.sdbor.edu/jumpstart/Pages/default.aspx

Tsui, L. (2007). Effective strategies to increase diversity in STEM fields: A review of the research literature. *The Journal of Negro Education, 76*(4), 555–581.

University of Kansas. (n.d.). *500 nations bridge collaboration: Haskell Indian Nations University/University of Kansas*. Retrieved from https://bridge.ku.edu/

University of New Mexico. (n.d.). *About NASTEM*. Retrieved from http://ess.unm.edu/ess-programs/nastem/index.html

University of New Mexico Health Sciences Center. (n.d.). *Center for Native American Health*. Retrieved from http://iikd.unm.edu/index.html

University of Oklahoma Department of Chemistry and Biochemistry. (n.d.). *K–12 outreach*. Retrieved from www.ou.edu/content/cas/chemistry/news-seminars-outreach/k-12-outreach.html

Watts, C. (2015, October 26). STEM and business day encourages American Indians to explore OU programs. *OU Daily*. Retrieved from http://www.oudaily.com/news/stem-and-business-day-encourages-american-indians-to-explore-ou/article_f8fb992e-799c-11e5-ad4b-a3d8745d0f09.html

6

RECRUITING AND SUPPORTING NURSING STUDENTS IN ALASKA

A Look at the Recruitment and Retention of Alaska Natives into Nursing (RRANN) Program at the University of Alaska Anchorage School of Nursing

Tina DeLapp, Jackie Pflaum, and Stephanie Sanderlin (Yupik/Unangan)

The Recruitment and Retention of Alaska Natives into Nursing (RRANN) program began in 1998 with federal grant funds to recruit and mentor Alaska Native and American Indian students in the pursuit of nursing degrees. RRANN was created in response to disparity. In 1998, Alaska Natives and American Indians made up nearly 20% of Alaska's population but less than 2% of the nursing workforce (DeLapp, Hautman, & Anderson, 2008). National statistics show the rate of American Indian and Alaska Native student enrollment in generic baccalaureate programs in nursing ranges from 0.7% between 2007 and 2009 to 0.6% in 2010 and 0.5% in 2014 (American Association of Colleges of Nursing, 2015). The National League for Nursing reports the national enrollment of American Indian or Alaska Native students in all basic RN programs at 1% (2013). Additionally, in 2013, only 1.6% of the national nursing workforce was American Indian or Alaska Native (Springer Publishing Company, 2015).

The RRANN program viewed the main barrier to Alaska Natives and American Indians entering nursing careers in Alaska as education: Alaska Natives and American Indians were not making it through nursing school. Most recently, the Lumina Foundation (2015) reported the college enrollment of 18- to 53-year-old Native Americans in Alaska at only 3.6% compared with 10.3% nationally and degree attainment rates among 25- to

64-year-old Native Americans in Alaska at 11.26%, well below all other population groups. The University of Alaska, Anchorage (UAA) is currently the only university in Alaska to offer a baccalaureate program in nursing (National League of Nursing, 2013). National calls to attract students from underrepresented groups into nursing is a high priority, and "nursing leaders recognize a strong connection between a culturally diverse nursing workforce and the ability to provide quality, culturally competent care" (American Association of Colleges of Nursing, 2015). The UAA and the RRANN program are uniquely placed to meet this challenge for Alaska Native communities.

In this chapter, we will examine four of the educational barriers confronting RRANN students at the UAA. We will also introduce the Ten Universal Alaska Native Values, compiled by the Alaska Native Knowledge Network (n.d.) at the University of Alaska, Fairbanks. These values provide a foundation for the program and provide the staff and administrators with culturally appropriate avenues for student support. Highlights of the program's success will conclude the chapter, and we encourage other Indigenous access programs to look to cultural values for guidance and vision.

RRANN is committed to increasing the number of Alaska Natives and American Indians graduating with an associate of applied sciences or baccalaureate of sciences nursing degree. RRANN is considered a major's group for students who are Alaska Native or American Indian, in good standing with the university, and enrolled in the School of Nursing classes. Students are required to apply to the program by completing an application form, which requires them to reflect on their cultural background and need for the program. Once selected to the program, RRANN helps students connect with on-campus housing, academic advising, and financial aid sources, including a scholarship program open only to RRANN students. Services provided also include tutoring, community building, advocacy, and the loaning of tools and required course supplies. The RRANN program asserts that working together and maintaining traditional values is the way to overcome barriers for Alaska Native and American Indian students in the university setting.

RRANN services are provided and delivered by a tutor coordinator and student success facilitators, whom many students refer to as "aunties at school." To maintain cultural integrity for students, student success facilitators ensure that RRANN remains guided by the Ten Universal Native Values (Alaska Native Knowledge Network, n.d.):

1. ***Show Respect to Others***—*Each Person Has a Special Gift*
2. ***Share What You Have***—*Giving Makes You Richer*
3. ***Know Who You Are***—*You Are a Reflection on Your Family*
4. ***Accept What Life Brings***—*You Cannot Control Many Things*

  5. *Have Patience—Some Things Cannot Be Rushed*
  6. *Live Carefully—What You Do Will Come Back to You*
  7. *Take Care of Others—You Cannot Live Without Them*
  8. *Honor Your Elders—They Show You the Way in Life*
  9. *Pray for Guidance—Many Things Are Not Known*
  10. *See Connections—All Things Are Related*

By using these values as a foundation and guide, RRANN is better equipped to support the unique needs and cultural backgrounds of its students. Students who were raised with and continue to live in traditional ways, those returning to traditional ways, and those beginning to define or explore them can all find something familiar in RRANN. RRANN makes every effort to employ student success facilitators who are Alaska Natives, have an understanding of rural Alaska, are shareholders in one or more of Alaska's Native corporations, and have experienced similar challenges throughout their educational paths. Student success facilitators serve as advocates, educators, guides, counselors, and mentors for students, and their first priority is providing one-to-one support for Native students starting with their college entrance as freshmen to their nursing degree completion and graduation. Student success facilitators are in a position to support students at each stage in their pursuit of the nursing degree because the RRANN program functions through the Universal Alaska Native Value: *Have Patience—Some Things Cannot Be Rushed.*

RRANN student success facilitators cite four challenges common to Native students pursuing nursing degrees: (a) student underpreparedness; (b) culture shock, homesickness, and loneliness; (c) unfamiliarity with higher education and UAA School of Nursing policies and procedures; and (d) financial need. The program has determined that responses to these challenges require four established and constant services: (a) tutoring; (b) meeting places, food, and cultural connections; (c) scholarship and lending programs; and (d) a strong Alaska Native Tribal Health Consortium (ANTHC) partnership. RRANN's understanding of student challenges and the program's established responses are modeled on the Universal Alaska Native Value: *See Connections—All Things Are Related.* A discussion of these student challenges and programmatic responses follows.

Student Underpreparedness

Student underpreparedness affects Alaska Native and American Indian students' entry into nursing school and their ability to perform academically when they do get there. Alaska Natives and American Indians have a distressing graduation rate within the total UAA population. Fewer than 5% of the students earning bachelor's degrees at UAA in 2007 were Alaska Native (Erickson & Hirshberg, 2008). The UAA estimates that retention rates for Alaska Native students run 10 to 15 percentage points below the university average, and roughly half of these students drop out within the first year (University of Alaska Anchorage, 2015). To help combat student academic underpreparedness, RRANN offers free tutoring to students at both the prenursing and nursing major levels.

Tutoring is specific to prerequisite prenursing courses and requisite nursing major courses such as anatomy and physiology, pathophysiology, and pharmacology. RRANN tutors are current UAA nursing students or recent graduates who work with professors to ensure that RRANN tutoring is aligned with course instruction. The student success facilitators inform the tutoring staff of coursework support needs by checking in on students regularly and assessing their current course grades. "To avoid creating the impression that Alaska Native/American Indian students have a special need for extra help" (DeLapp, Hautman, & Anderson, 2008, p. 295), which many early RRANN students feared would marginalize them within the student body and create barriers to integration into the program, all nursing students are welcome in tutoring and are encouraged to participate. Tutoring is offered in student cohorts to blend students' academic and social structures. RRANN believes in community and in helping students build networks that serve them as students persisting together and as future professionals teaming together. This cohort model allows RRANN students to learn from both their tutors and fellow nursing students and shows them that labs and classrooms aren't the only places where instruction occurs. For RRANN students, teaching and learning are reinforced as a way of life.

After receiving instruction from professors and support through tutoring, students are able to work with their peers and are assured they are studying the correct material in appropriate ways. This expresses the Universal Alaska Native Values: ***Live Carefully***—*What You Do Will Come Back to You* and ***Show Respect to Others***—*Each Person Has a Special Gift.*

Culture Shock, Homesickness, and Loneliness

Culture shock, homesickness, and loneliness negatively impact students' functionality and are enough to drive students out of formal Western education. After interviewing Alaska Native and American Indian first-time first-year students who had left school, UAA Native Student Services found that the primary reason for leaving was "personal reasons" (Erickson & Hirshberg, 2008). The students interviewed did not see their traditional values reflected in the UAA and greater Anchorage communities, and this made them feel out of place. Students cited feeling that they had nothing to give and, therefore, no place in the community. Lack of access to traditional foods and gatherings further intensified feelings of confusion, isolation, strangeness, and worthlessness. As a result, students often found their cultural identity threatened in this environment.

One program response to this cultural conflict comes through the Universal Alaska Native Value: **Know Who You Are**—*You Are a Reflection of Your Family.* This value is reflected in RRANN's enrollment procedures. In applying for enrollment, prospective RRANN students answer the following questions:

1. How does your cultural background motivate you to pursue success?
2. How will your participation enrich the RRANN program?

These questions allow students to present the strengths of their families and/or communities along with the valuable background and experiences students offer. This differs from other academic and scholarship application questions, where students are tasked with primarily discussing their academic goals and needs. The RRANN application allows students to present and reflect on their cultural identity as an asset to a UAA program. Students have access to each other's statements to demonstrate that they are part of a community that shares traditions, values, connections, and inspiration.

To further combat culture shock, homesickness, and loneliness, RRANN also hosts monthly gatherings featuring guest speakers and traditional and meaningful foods donated by Alaska Native hunters, fishers, and gatherers. These gatherings provide an opportunity for students to come together to enjoy foods they know and don't have access to on campus. They also provide an opportunity for students to learn from guest speakers chosen to benefit them as students, future nurses, and Native people. The gatherings also function as a council where students can raise concerns, express needs, share resources, and encourage each other. This approach supports the Universal Alaska Native Values: **Share What You Have**—*Giving Makes You Richer* and **Take Care of Others**—*You Cannot Live Without Them.*

Unfamiliarity With Higher Education and UAA School of Nursing Policies and Procedures

Approximately 90% of RRANN students are first-generation college students (Alaska Center for Rural Health at the University of Alaska, Anchorage, n.d.). Many are the first in their families to finish high school. This often means that complex and bureaucratic processes, such as applying for financial aid, filing academic appeals, course and degree planning, and course registration, often leave students anxious and overwhelmed. Like other first-generation college students, too often RRANN students have to navigate these difficult processes without family support (McDonough, 1997). RRANN responds by assisting students one on one with any and all processes, including inviting students into the office to complete online documents with the student success facilitators. RRANN student success facilitators also maintain a strong relationship with the UAA School of Nursing Office of Student Services by working closely with School of Nursing advisers to help students understand university policies and procedures. The student success facilitators have direct access to the personnel who schedule tutoring space, present official Financial Aid Appeals to the UAA Financial Aid Office, submit Satisfactory Academic Progress plans and documentation, and verify academic status for externships, clinicals, scholarships, and other awards.

The UAA School of Nursing does not have any instructors or administrators who identify as Alaska Native or American Indian. As a result, student success facilitators work to bridge gaps in communication, promote awareness of Native students' needs and learning styles, and mediate conflicts. Student success facilitators also access course syllabi to review with students and clarify individual course procedures and requirements, required texts, assessment schedules and point values, and project completion dates. Student success facilitators occasionally attend class sessions to maintain familiarity with classroom structures, note taking, participation expectations and requirements, and teaching styles. This ensures that student success facilitators are able to work with students to understand and clarify the details of courses. More important, it allows the facilitators to mentor students on ways to better understand instructor personalities and preferences so students are empowered and equipped to individually approach instructors and self-advocate.

To ensure that students are aware and ready for deadlines such as add/drop dates, bookstore refund windows, clinical placement, and graduation applications, RRANN provides yearly planners preprinted with all UAA events, dates, and deadlines. Student success facilitators e-mail students with reminders of each important item and post them on the RRANN Facebook page. All RRANN students are able to post on the RRANN Facebook page, so they can add any reminders they feel are important. They can also network with each other to trade tasks and group errands, which saves individual trips to offices spread throughout the UAA campus and Anchorage community. RRANN staff and students work together to get everything done in line with the Universal Alaska Native Values: ***Take Care of Others***—*You Cannot Live Without Them* and ***Show Respect to Others***—*Each Person Has a Special Gift.*

Financial Need

According to the University of Alaska Anchorage's Institute of Social and Economic Research, the median income of Alaska Native households is only two-thirds that of all Alaska households and is close to 20% below the national average. Further, Alaska Natives experience more unemployment and poverty than other Americans. The unemployment rate for Alaska Natives is 16%, nearly twice the national average of 8.1% in August 2012, and 22% of Alaska Natives live below the poverty line, nearly twice the national average of 12% (Martin & Hill, 2009).

Students in the RRANN program have the advantage of employment advising and job placement assistance upon graduation and licensure. The ANTHC partners with the RRANN program to prepare graduating students to seek nursing jobs at the Alaska Native Medical Center (ANMC) in Anchorage, Alaska. Senior nurse recruiters from ANTHC meet with graduating students in the familiar setting of the RRANN offices to review job applications, resumes, and cover letters and provide information on what to expect in the interview process as well as upon entering the ANMC workforce if hired as an employee. Upon completing an application, senior nurse recruiters fast-track RRANN applicants to nurse managers throughout the hospital campus for review. This means students in the RRANN program experience less anxiety about their eventual job search, and they are assured that the health workplace is eager to receive them. It also gives them a way to plan financially because they have access to salary figures at ANMC.

In response to student financial need, RRANN provides tools that nursing students need, such as Smart Pens, stethoscopes, watches, and scrubs, saving students, on average, more than $500. This matters greatly because the demands of nursing school do not allow many students to work outside class. Money is especially tight for them, but due to RRANN's assistance, students have the tools they need when they need them without the burden of spending their limited monies or incurring additional debts. RRANN also has a scholarship program exclusive to Alaska Native and American Indian nursing students, awarding each student up to $1,000 per term. There are no restrictions on use of the scholarship award; students may use the monies for life expenses such as child care, grocery bills, and car repair. This funding is intended to help students overcome the barrier of financial need, especially when they are supporting families while attending school.

Scholarships are awarded to nursing majors enrolled in the RRANN program who are taking a minimum of six credits. Recipients must maintain a 2.0 or higher GPA and attend a minimum of one RRANN gathering per term. Students maintain accountability for their awards by submitting a thank you letter to the program, explaining how they have used their funds. Recipients are also required to give a nonmonetary gift, such as RRANN newsletter content, photos of themselves participating in school or cultural activities, or serving as public speakers at UAA fund raising and support events on behalf of Native students. These requirements also serve an additional purpose by providing student success facilitators with the means to assess students' mental and spiritual health. Students who are not completing RRANN scholarship requirements are typically experiencing problems, including emotional and spiritual health struggles that may require intervention, which students may be reluctant or unable to express directly in other ways. The RRANN scholarship requirements are in line with the Universal Alaska Native Values: ***Share What You Have****—Giving Makes You Richer* and ***Take Care of Others****—You Cannot Live Without Them.*

Conclusion

Providing culturally relevant health care is not a matter of political correctness; it is often a matter of life and death. When cultural competency is missing from health care, important information is not communicated, symptoms of illness are overlooked or misinterpreted, and patient outcome suffers (RRANN's founder, Tina DeLapp, personal communication, 1998).

Native students are honored by this statement and committed to addressing a need that only they can fill. RRANN is a place in higher education where Alaska Natives and American Indians fit because of who they are and where they come from. In 2006, UAA ranked seventh in the nation for Alaska Native and American Indian students earning bachelor's degrees in various health-related programs. Sixty percent of these graduates were RRANN students (Alaska Center for Rural Health at the University of Alaska, Anchorage, n.d.).

RRANN's work has made a difference. The graduation rate for Alaska Native nursing majors in the RRANN program is 83% compared with 10% for Alaska Native students not in the RRANN program and 56% for Alaska Native students at the UAA overall (Alaska Center for Rural Health at the University of Alaska, Anchorage, n.d.). RRANN graduates also have notable passing rates for the National Council Licensure Examination (NCLEX), the exam required to obtain a Registered Nurse (RN) license and begin work as a professional nurse. In 2014, upon first attempt, RRANN graduates passed the NCLEX and became licensed RNs at the same rate as their UAA School of Nursing peers: above 80% (RRANN, 2015).

Students in the RRANN program receive help and guidance in critical areas both in and outside of academic concerns. They are supported as a community and as individuals so they are not alone in struggles and unforeseen crises. It is a whole-person approach aligned with the Universal Alaska Native Value: ***Accept What Life Brings***—*You Cannot Control Many Things.* "Since 1998, RRANN has helped over 270 AN/AI students graduate from the UAA School of Nursing [and] currently assists over 300 nurse majors and pre-majors on University of Alaska campuses statewide" (UAA School of Nursing, n.d.). These students emerge as strong and valued individuals capable of literally saving lives and contributing to healthier communities and families.

References

Alaska Center for Rural Health at the University of Alaska, Anchorage. (n.d.). *Program evaluation student survey spring 2010.*

Alaska Native Knowledge Network. (n.d.). *Alaska Native values for curriculum.* Retrieved from www.ankn.uaf.edu/ANCR/Values/

American Association of Colleges of Nursing. (2013). *Race/ethnicity data on students enrolled in nursing programs: 10-year data on minority students in baccalaureate and graduate programs.* Retrieved from www.aacn.nche.edu/research-data/EthnicityTbl.pdf

American Association of Colleges of Nursing. (2015). *Fact sheet: Enhancing diversity in the nursing workforce.* Retrieved from www.aacn.nche.edu/media-relations/fact-sheets/enhancing-diversity

DeLapp, T., Hautman, M. A., & Anderson, M. S. (2008). Recruitment and retention of Alaska Natives in Nursing (RRANN). *Journal of Nursing Education, 47*(7), 293–297.

Erickson, D., & Hirshberg, D. (2008). Alaska Native graduates of UAA: What can they tell us? *University of Alaska's Institute of Social and Economic Research, Understanding Alaska Research Summary No. 11.* Retrieved from www.iser.uaa.alaska.edu/Publications/researchsumm/AKNativegrad.pdf

Lumina Foundation. (2015). *A stronger nation through higher education: Ten-year time horizon brings Goal 2025 into sharp focus.* Indianapolis, IN: Author.

Martin, S., & Hill, A. (2009). The changing economic status of Alaska Natives 1970–2007. *University of Alaska's Institute of Social and Economic Research Summary No. 5.* Retrieved from www.iser.uaa.alaska.edu/Publications/webnote/WebNote5.pdf

McDonough, P. M. (1997). *Choosing colleges: How social class and schools structure opportunity.* Albany, NY: SUNY Press.

National League of Nursing. (2013). *Annual survey of Schools of Nursing, fall 2012.* Retrieved from www.nin.org.research/slides/index.htm

Springer Publishing Company. (2015). *Nursing statistics: Nurses by race and ethnicity.*
Retrieved from http://minoritynurse.com/wp-content/uploads/2015/01/3-03.png

University of Alaska Anchorage. (2015). *Performance '12.* Retrieved from www
.uaa.alaska.edu/institutionaleffectiveness/upload/performance-12-for-web.pdf

UAA School of Nursing (n.d.) *Recruiting and retention of Alaska natives into nursing (RRANN).* Retrieved from https://www.uaa.alaska.edu/academics/college-of-health/departments/school-of-nursing/rrann/

COREY'S STORY

Corey Still (Keetoowah Cherokee)

As I reflect over the past couple of years and my own academic journey, I can honestly say that I may be the most surprised that I am where I am. At the time of this writing, I have been out of high school for more than seven years. Within seven years, so much can change. The fact that I'm even being asked to write about my journey is a testament in and of itself, but it's really not just my journey. It's a journey of many reflected through my eyes. Seven years ago, if you had told me I would be working toward a PhD, I wouldn't know whether I would laugh or look at you as if you were crazy. I assumed that the completion of my undergraduate degree would mark the completion of my academic journey. However, I was mistaken. When I began to process how I wanted to approach talking about this journey, I knew that I wanted to discuss my access to graduate school in a way that reflected the gratitude and appreciation my family and I have for the organizations and individuals that have supported me in my endeavors. Before I dive into too much about my current journey and the access I was afforded, I would be remiss if I didn't first acknowledge who I am and where I come from.

I am Keetoowah Cherokee and the third of four children of Stella Still-Campbell and Darrell Campbell. I am the grandson of the late John and Betty Still, the great-grandson of the late Bessie Thompson, and the great-nephew of Eva Thompson. I was born and raised in and around the area of Tahlequah, Oklahoma, and was fortunate to have a family that ensured I had a cultural upbringing. As a first-generation college student, there were many hesitations about me leaving my community. However, the most challenging barrier for that journey was finding the funding to attend college. When I began to research colleges and universities that I wanted to attend, the largest factor I took into consideration was their cost of attendance. My family does not come from a place of privilege. I was always taught from an early age that I needed to work for everything that I wanted in life, whether that be money to go out, new clothes, or anything that I needed to buy. So when I began to approach the prospect of going to college, I knew that if I wanted to attend, I would need to work to get there.

During this time, I experienced my relationship with a program that would eventually provide me the most access to graduate school. In spring 2009, I was named a recipient of the Gates Millennium Scholars Program scholarship. That day changed my life. It opened the doors to a world I thought I would never be privileged enough to walk in. The Gates program provided me with the unique ability to never have to worry about how I would pay for school. Even better, it ensured that my schooling would never become a burden to my family. There are not enough words to describe the gratitude my family and I have for this program. It has allowed me to earn my undergraduate degree and has opened the door for me to obtain a master's degree and, finally, pursue a PhD.

As I continue on through this journey, I have been extremely lucky to cross paths with a number of people without whom I could never imagine my life. The role of mentors in my journey may be the biggest factor to my pathway to graduate school. As an undergraduate planning to go into my master's program, I remember three influential faculty members who motivated me to go beyond what I thought my terminal degree would be: Heather Shotton, Barbara Hobson, and Jerry Bread. What can I say about these three professors? They made my undergraduate life a struggle, but without their support, I never would have found my interest in research. I consider these three individuals the primary reason that I am in graduate school. The support they provided for me outside of just academia is something I will cherish for the remainder of my life. I especially recall one time, a few weeks before graduation, I was struggling with where I was going to go for my master's program. I sat with Professor Shotton and was talking through my options. I was really missing home and the connection to my community that initially pushed me to pursue higher education. Finally, after a long conversation, I remember her looking at me and telling me in a frank way to go home. She supported my decision to go and accept my admission into a local, regional institution. She told me that my connection to my family was by far more important to my education than where I received my education. I cherish those words. I consider these three mentors a part of my family; they are my auntie, my mom, and my uncle.

While speaking on the idea of mentors, it would be wrong of me not to mention Professors Jennifer McCann and Susan Frusher. These two professors were my anchors in my master's program. I worked for Professor McCann, who provided me with opportunities to present at a number of conferences, and she encouraged me to take my work outside of my comfort zone. Professor Frusher was my academic adviser and chair of my thesis committee. She was always on me, making sure I was where I needed to be, and was my strongest advocate with the graduate college. I'm still not sure who was worried more about me finishing my master's degree, her or me. I recall us meeting in her office and her asking me question after question regarding my writing and research. I cherish those meetings because they kept me on track and kept me focused on my end goal.

I never would have made it this far without acknowledging two groups of people that have been there with me throughout my entire process. The first group is my brothers of Sigma Nu Alpha Gamma, Inc., a Native American fraternity founded at the University of Oklahoma. I'm not sure whether they will know the true impact they have had on my life. When I was ready to throw in the towel and give up, my brothers literally stood in the way of my truck so I couldn't leave. They give me strength every day. As the only boy out of all my siblings, they became my true brothers. I can never repay the debt I owe them for being there for me.

Finally, there is my family. I would not be here doing what I am doing without them. I never could have accomplished what I set out to do without them. During the darkest moments in my journey, my nieces and nephews have pulled me through. I think about them and the life I want them to lead. I know that I cannot make their path smooth and free of obstacles, but I can at least rid their path of some of the obstacles that I faced, just as my mentors removed some obstacles in my path. I do what I do for them. I hope that one day they will understand why I had to be away so much and that one day they can read this and know that at my core they are the reason I pushed myself so hard to achieve a graduate education—to show them that if I can do it, they can too. Many people have impacted my journey. There are not enough words to express how I feel for them all. So I will simply say this, *Wado*, Thank you.

7

THE EVOLUTION OF NATIVE EDUCATION LEADERSHIP PROGRAMS

Learning From the Past, Leading for the Future

Susan C. Faircloth (Coharie Tribe of North Carolina) and Robin Minthorn (Kiowa/Nez Perce/Umatilla/Assiniboine)

I n this chapter, we discuss the evolution of educational leadership programs for American Indian and Alaska Native students. The emergence of programs aimed at preparing Native principals, superintendents, and other school leaders began in earnest in the 1960s and 1970s with the establishment of educational leadership preparation programs at Arizona State University, Harvard University, The Pennsylvania State University, and the University of Minnesota (Farquhar & Martin, 1972). As the following timeline illustrates, efforts to increase the number of Native educational leaders were spawned, in large part, by social and political unrest and a desire to return control of Indian education into the hands of Native peoples and their communities. Although these programs have made significant impacts across the nation, there is an ongoing need for Native educational leaders at the K–12 levels as well as across the educational spectrum, including higher education.

Timeline

The 1960s and 1970s marked the beginning of an era of "self-determination," a period during which Native communities were emboldened to reclaim the right to determine and direct the education of their tribal citizens in ways that embraced and fostered their cultural and linguistic diversity and heritage

(Szasz, 1999). This fight for truly self-determined education played out at the K–12 level as well as within the higher education arena (Oppelt, 1990), creating opportunities for Native peoples. As Wright and Tierney (1991) argue, "American Indians must have opportunities to enter the higher education arena on their own terms—to encounter challenge without tragedy and triumph without co-optation" (p. 18). Key events are noted in brief in the following:

1964   The Economic Opportunity Act, signed into law in 1964 by President Johnson, made it the official policy of the U.S. government "to eliminate the paradox of poverty in the midst of plenty in this Nation by opening to everyone the opportunity for education and training, the opportunity to work, and the opportunity to live in decency and dignity" (Prucha, 1984, p. 1093). This act paved the way for the establishment of Native educational leadership preparation programs within colleges and universities.

1966   The first American Indian community controlled school was established on the Navajo Reservation (Rough Rock Demonstration School), followed by four other community schools. By 1978, there were 34 Indian community schools (Lomawaima & McCarty, 2002).

1968   The first tribally controlled college, Navajo Community College (now known as Diné College), was established on the Navajo Reservation (Stein, 1999).

1969   The landmark report, *Indian education: A national tragedy a national challenge* (also known as the Kennedy Report), was published. This report "detailed the singular failings of existing approaches to educating American Indians and identified many of the special needs and circumstances of American Indian and Alaska Native students" (Snipp, 2014, p. 361).

1970   President Nixon announced the beginning of increased local control of Indian education (Lomawaima & McCarty, 2002).

1970   The National Indian Education Association (NIEA[1]) was established.

1972   The Indian Education Act was passed. This Act established the Office of Indian Education within the U.S. Department of Education and the National Advisory Council on Indian Education (NACIE) (National Advisory Council on Indian Education, 1975).

1975   The Indian Self-Determination and Education Assistance Act (PL 93-638) was passed, allowing the Bureau of Indian Affairs (BIA) to contract with tribes for the provision of education services. In issuing this law, President Nixon wrote, "It is long past time that the Indian policies of the Federal government began to recognize and build upon the capacities and insights of the Indian people. Both as a matter of justice and as a matter of enlightened social policy, we must begin to act on the basis of what the Indians themselves have long been telling us. The time has come to break decisively with the past and to create the conditions for a new era in which the Indian future is determined by Indian acts and Indian decisions" (Reyhner, 2006).

1978   PL 95-561 (Education Amendments of 1978) was passed, requiring American Indian parents and tribes to be involved in the spending of impact aid monies—funds designated for geographic locations and related entities, including reservations, to offset the loss of the federal tax base in these areas.

The Establishment of Native Education Leadership Programs Within Non-Native Colleges and Universities (NNCUs)

In 1970, four university programs were established with funding from the Office of Economic Opportunity and the BIA to provide leadership development for American Indian and Alaska Native students. These programs were housed at Arizona State University, Harvard University, the University of Minnesota, and The Pennsylvania State University. Establishment of these programs was due in part to the Indian self-determination movement, which sought increased local/tribal control of Indian education (Faircloth & Tippeconnic, 2013) and a national movement to expand the pool of talented American Indian and Alaska Native educational leaders (Farquhar & Martin, 1972).

Although each of these programs was successful in its own right, the American Indian Leadership Program (AILP), originally named The Penn State Native American Indian Administrator program, was the only one to offer administrator preparation programs for Natives on a continuous basis for more than 40 years (Faircloth & Tippeconnic, 2015). Some of the key features of this program included the scheduling of a seminar specifically designed to build a sense of cohesion among the group, a paid internship and field-based experience, and travel support. Faculty from outside the Division of Education Policy Studies (e.g., rural sociology, human development, regional planning, economics, history, and anthropology) also expressed a willingness to work with the program (Lynch, 1973).

During their tenure in this program, the initial participants attempted to change the culture and operation of the BIA by encouraging the Bureau to

adopt individualized instruction and differentiated staffing, involving citizen groups in Title I program approval, evaluating peripheral dormitories,
laying the groundwork for moving of district from an all-Anglo board to
Indian participation by convincing the Indian population that they had
the right to vote in school board elections, working with Native village
leadership in planning schools activities, and working with tribal leaders
and tribal educational agencies in reorganizing the structure of education.
(Lynch, 1973, p. 8)

The AILP's inaugural director, Pat Lynch, argued that this program not
only changed the participants and the bureau, but it also had an impact on the
university by forcing it to reenvision the ways in which it went about recruiting, retaining, and instructing American Indian and Alaska Native students.
The AILP also provided a unique opportunity for the Education Policy Studies
Division, in which the AILP was housed, to rethink its selection and admissions criteria beyond its traditional focus on standardized test scores and GPAs.
By considering other criteria, the university "verbalize[d] a willingness to take a
risk, [and] set loose from the system somehow" (Lynch, 1973, p. 10). The first
group of students was also instrumental in selecting subsequent cohort members. Throughout this process, the students were adamant that they wanted
future students to demonstrate involvement in and commitment to tribes and
tribal communities. Other notable highlights of the AILP include the hiring of
the first Navajo professor of educational administration to work with this program and collaboration with the University Council for Educational Administration in an attempt to bring national prominence to the need to train Native
educational leaders. According to Faircloth and Tippeconnic (2013), "Since
1970, the AILP has graduated more than 220 American Indian and Alaska
Native students who have earned their master's or doctoral degrees in educational administration and educational leadership" (p. 481).

Although the emergence of Native educational leadership preparation
programs was a response in part to larger social, political, and economic
movements taking place across Indian country, these programs were also
heavily influenced by the fact that traditional Western conceptions of
leadership development were not sufficient for those working in and with
Native schools and communities. Warner and Grint (2006) cite differences
between American Indian and Western conceptions of leadership; they
also cite "the historical dearth of research into American Indian leadership"
(p. 229). Western approaches emphasize position, whereas American Indian
approaches emphasize persuasion. Western approaches focus on the individual, whereas American Indian approaches focus on leadership that fits the
particular situation or context and how their leadership can best serve community members. Austin (2005) argued,

The teachers and administrators that American Indian education needs most are those capable of using American Indian cultures and traditional teaching methods to motivate and educate American Indian children. We know that local control of schools promotes community and parent involvement in education. The school becomes the hub of community life on a reservation. (p. 45)

Austin (2005) went on to write that "American Indian teachers and administrators who know their cultures and apply them in the schools and tribal communities are the key to local control of schools and American Indian education shedding its assimilationist practices" (p. 45). This passage speaks to the importance of working intentionally and proactively to recruit, train, and hire leaders who know, value, and enact Indigenous culture, practices, and beliefs.

Impact of Native Educational Leadership Programs

According to Leitka and colleagues (1975), graduates of Native educational leadership programs

> have made an important beginning towards a cadre of trained education professionals available to Indian communities and to programs serving Indian people. These efforts represent a positive step toward Indian self-determination in the field of education; particularly in the role of management of school programs. (Foreword)

The collective impact of the graduates of these programs continues to be felt today, as noted by Warner and Grint (2006), who describe that the graduates of the American Indian Leadership Program at Penn State are often referred to as belonging to the "Penn State Mafia" (Warner & Grint, 2006, p. 234). Programs such as the Penn State AILP greatly impacted the advancement of Native education leaders and researchers, who went on to return to their communities or enter educational administration positions across the country.

Ongoing Need for Culturally Relevant Leadership Preparation

Although the number of Native educational leadership preparation programs grew as a result of the self-determination movement of the 1960s and 1970s, many of these programs operated from dominant Western leadership paradigms, which failed to fully acknowledge or incorporate traditional Native leadership teachings and practices. Warner and Grint (2006) characterize such approaches as "simultaneously decontextualized and individualized" (p. 234). Research also suggests, "Almost all of the educational leadership programs in the United States approach leadership preparation using leadership constructs derived from the dominant Western paradigm" (Henderson, Carjuzaa, & Ruff, 2015, p. 212).

In recent years, administrator preparation programs have begun responding to the call to develop more culturally relevant leadership preparation programs. For example, the American Indian Administrator Education Program: Preparing for the Future—South Dakota State University, Oglala Lakota College and Sinte Gleska University—prepared school leaders for the elementary and secondary levels (Mills & Amiotte, 1996). This three-year initiative (1994–1997), funded by the Bush Foundation, awarded master's degrees in Educational Administration. Courses were offered at a centralized location between the Pine Ridge and Rosebud reservations, on the weekends, and were portfolio-based. A similar program, Model for American Indian School Administrators (MAISA), funded by a personnel development grant from the U.S. Department of Education's Office of Indian Education, was founded at New Mexico State University. According to Christman, Guillory, Fairbanks, and Gonzalez (2008), this program addressed the need for non-traditional administrator preparation programs for aspiring American Indian educational leaders. MAISA was innovative in that it utilized interactive television, face-to-face instruction, and summer residency-based programming on campus and was developed based on the principle of reciprocity. Project staff conducted research with project participants to determine the types of supports that were helpful to these students as they completed their degree program, the impact of the program on students' long- and short-term goals, and the lessons learned for the university. Five themes were identified: (a) the importance of relationships, (b) external influences on student degree completion, (c) impact of the program in preparing participants to become school leaders, (d) students' altruistic view of their calling to help others, and (e) the importance of family (Christman et al., 2008). Project staff also noted the importance of establishing a cohort, incorporating culturally based readings and other assignments, and hiring American Indian faculty to teach courses in the degree program. This important program feature gives tribal members the opportunity to see themselves in leadership positions. Another key element of this program was the extent to which program staff paid attention to the unique needs and circumstances of students who were not on campus full time.

In both of the programs cited earlier, Native faculty and staff played key roles in the design and delivery of the degree programs and related experiences. As future programs are established, it will be important to draw on the lessons learned from these initiatives and ensure that Native faculty and staff are involved. Unfortunately, the small numbers of Native faculty make this goal difficult to achieve. As reported by the U.S. Department of Education's National Center for Education Statistics (2015), less than 1% of all full-time faculty in postsecondary institutions identify as American Indian or Alaska Native.

Need for Increased Indigenous Leadership in Higher Education

Although colleges and universities have attempted to respond to the need for Indigenous educational leaders, these efforts have not been sufficient to meet the increasing need for Indigenous educational leaders at the postsecondary level. As more and more Native students pursue higher education, it will be imperative that they see Native educational leaders in colleges and universities across the nation, including NNCUs, as well as tribal colleges and universities (TCUs). Fortunately, the groundwork has already begun to be laid. For example, in 2002, the Kellogg Foundation funded an initiative, in collaboration with the Alliance for Equity in Higher Education, to train aspiring leaders from minority-serving institutions (MSIs), including TCUs, historically Black colleges and universities, and Hispanic-serving institutions. Through this program, fellows were paired with the president of an MSI for a year-long internship. The goal was "to prepare the next generation of senior administrators" (León & Nevarez, 2007, p. 371). Throughout this initiative, particular attention was given "to the critical dimensions of context, process, and succession" (Merisotis, 2005, p. 4) as they relate to the individual MSI. Unfortunately, funding for this initiative ended in 2006.

Already, the role of tribal colleges is evident in the growing body of research and literature on Indigenous leadership in higher education, which centers primarily on the role of TCU presidents and their perspectives on leadership. For example, Johnson (1997) describes the Osah Gan Gio Model of leadership development, which highlights five roles of leaders: (a) sharing a commitment to serve their community, (b) claiming their voice for themselves and their community, (c) demonstrating and modeling ways that education is key to cultural survival and self-determination, (d) traveling across boundaries to understand and bridge relationship with others who are different from themselves, and (e) continuously nurturing their inner spirit and sustaining their soul through balance in their lives. Warner and Gipp (2009) pointed out the role of the American Indian Higher Education Consortium (AIHEC) in developing future TCU presidents. More recently, Pidgeon (2012) discussed Indigenous leadership in higher education from a macrolevel, not specific to TCUs, but as she has seen it displayed for Aboriginal people in Canada and the experiences they have in seeing leaders as relations and warriors. Specifically, she highlights Canada's Supporting Aboriginal Graduate Enhancement program, which demonstrates a community effort to provide support and mentorship to undergraduate students as they find their pathways in their fields and professions and transition to graduate studies.

Although these publications highlight Indigenous leadership in higher education by focusing on the experiences of TCU presidents, Indigenous leadership at a macrolevel, and research surrounding Native student leadership perspectives and development, there is an ongoing need to conduct research and publish literature specific to Indigenous leadership in all facets of higher education. Such research will help to illuminate the way in which Native educational leaders have been able to successfully navigate the academic culture of higher education while also working to maintain their own traditional cultures, identities, and notions of effective leadership.

The Future of Native Educational Leadership Programs

Although many programs have been designed to increase the number of aspiring Native American educational leaders, the need for such initiatives persists. Programs such as the American Indian Leadership Program at Penn State have made an impact by increasing the number of Native educational leaders in the K–12 system. Unfortunately, programs such as this have often required participants to leave their home or tribal communities to pursue a graduate or terminal degree. This has created tensions for many graduates who seek to return home following completion of their degree program but who encounter a disconnect between themselves and their home communities when they do return. Bourdieu (1977; cited in Perna & Titus, 2005) refers to this as a loss of one's social capital—the social networks and relationships within the community—and/or cultural capital—"the system of attributes, such as language skills, cultural knowledge, and mannerisms, that is derived in part from one's parents and that defines an individual's class status" (Bourdieu, 1986; cited in Perna & Titus, 2005, p. 488). Fortunately, with grant funding, some programs have made good traction in creating cohorts or implementing programs to fill a need in an area near a university or college.

One of the greatest barriers to developing and sustaining leadership programs designed specifically for aspiring Native educational leaders is the lack of sufficient funding for the operation and maintenance of such programs.

The goal of the original funding for programs, such as the AILP at Penn State, was for colleges and universities to institutionalize these programs and make them an integral part of the core mission of these institutions. However, in many cases, colleges and universities have continued to depend on external grant funding to sustain these programs. Some might argue that this calls into question the true institutional commitment to the development of Native educational leaders. Another tension associated with educational leadership programs is the silo nature of higher education programs. Traditionally, such programs have forced many aspiring school leaders to focus on either K–12 education or higher education, rather than recognizing that learning is a lifelong process, and a successful model of school leadership may in fact be tied to one's ability to create and sustain an educational pipeline from K–12 to postsecondary education. Additionally, previous models have also failed to fully account for the need for highly skilled leaders to work with TCUs.

The Native American Leadership in Education Program

One example of how Native educational leadership programs are building their capacity to do this important work is demonstrated in the increasing presence of Native faculty in NNCUs who are being empowered to develop and create Native-focused educational leadership programs. For instance, at the University of New Mexico, a cohort-based doctoral degree (EdD) in Native American Leadership in Education (NALE) has been developed. Instead of developing this program based solely on the expertise of faculty within the program, the university made a concerted effort to obtain perspectives of tribal communities and Native educational leaders, in both K–12 and higher education. Only after meetings with these tribal entities and the establishment of an advisory board was the curriculum for this cohort-based program created. A community advisory board was seen as an essential component to hold the program accountable to the communities it serves and to provide the program an opportunity for continued follow-up and feedback for accountability and transparency. The community advisory board is made up of stakeholders from community, university, and state constituencies, including the Secretary of New Mexico Indian Education and representatives from Native charter schools, TCUs, and Native faculty.

Once the curriculum was formed, Native faculty across the university and within the community were identified to teach the courses. The university felt it was important to create a program that addressed the current cultural and educational needs within tribal communities to ensure that the curriculum consistently incorporated an Indigenous perspective in the content and delivery of each course. An essential part of ensuring that the program is meeting its objective is maintaining tribal and community engagement, which involves follow-up meetings with leaders, tribes, and other stakeholders to discuss lessons learned and recommendations for moving forward. These meetings also allow the program to provide updates every semester on the cohort via newsletters and brochures given to the community, and they also provide an avenue to recruit Native American academic mentors who have doctoral degrees from the community.

The first NALE cohort began its doctoral journey in the 2016–2017 academic year, following intentional efforts to develop the cohort in collaboration with the tribal communities of New Mexico and to increase the number of Native American educational leaders in K–12 and higher education across the state. During the first year, seven Native American students were inducted into the program in the presence of their partners, children, parents, sisters, brothers, grandparents, grandchildren, and other relatives. This induction acknowledged the doctoral journey as a family's journey, not just one person's journey. To keep family members connected to the journey, the program includes family gatherings every semester. Another unique aspect of the program is the lack of a required in-residence status. As such, courses are offered in a hybrid format, both online and in person. In this approach, the program understands the importance of enabling Native students to remain in full-time positions within their communities.

In the summer of their first year, visits with tribal education leaders and communities were conducted by the NALE cohort. Plans to visit with communities that were not included in the first summer are set for the following summer. This ensures that the program accurately highlights Indigenous-based education and connects students to communities to build relationships and networks of support during the program. To make the program more accessible to Native students, the delivery of the program is also determined each year from feedback received from the current cohort. The NALE students are also given opportunities to present on their experiences in the program to underscore the importance of sharing their lived experiences while gaining experience with professional presentations in Native-based educational conferences.

Native American Higher Education Leadership Programs

The NALE doctoral program is one example of a Native educational leadership program that has been developed and offered to Native students through intentional, community-informed, and community-based outreach. The program demonstrates an emerging dynamic in Native educational leadership programs—being more accessible to tribal communities and being intentional in cocreating curriculum and course delivery. As mentioned earlier, there is an increasing need for educational leadership programs that are not K–12 specific, but broader in scope, in order to develop higher education administrators. For example, there is a need to prepare leaders who are able to work effectively in TCUs across the United States and Canada. Currently, 34 TCUs are regular members of AIHEC, 3 TCUs are associate members, and 1 TCU is an international member (American Indian Higher Education Consortium, 2014). TCUs are in need of succession planning for current presidents and administrators to help build future generations of leaders. There is also an increasing need to incorporate the development of Native higher education and student affairs administrators in NNCUs.

In recent years, a number of NNCUs (e.g., Arizona State University, University of Arizona, University of Idaho, Washington State University, University of Oregon, University of New Mexico, University of Oklahoma, and the American Indian Center at the University of North Carolina Chapel Hill) have created opportunities for Native American educational leaders to reach broader positions of leadership through tribal liaison positions and Native American student center director positions. Currently, there are no academic programs or cohorts in Native educational leadership in higher education, with the exception of an American Indian Higher Education certificate through the American Indian Studies program at the University of Arizona (University of Arizona, 2014).

Recommendations and Next Steps

If we are to see an increase in the number and type of programs aimed at preparing Native educational leaders, then mainstream higher education institutions need to redefine the way in which academic programs are designed and formed, particularly within educational leadership programs. In addition to structural and logistical redesign, these programs will need to undergo a cultural reformation that enables them to better understand and appreciate the lived experiences of Native peoples, their educational leadership needs and desires, and the communities Native educational leaders hope to serve. This means reshaping our approaches to leadership development so that we acknowledge and respect the values of leaders who are tribally and community based.

Recommendations for Future Research

Although anecdotal evidence suggests that the number of American Indian students pursuing degrees in educational administration and leadership-related fields has increased since the emergence of Native-focused leadership preparation programs in the 1970s, ongoing research is required to document evidence of the impact of these leaders on Native student performance at the PK–12 levels. It is also important for educational leadership programs to incorporate a P–20 focus and to study the impact of graduates within their respective communities, as well as within Native education organizations. This includes advocacy and leadership at the local, state, tribal, national, and international levels. As we continue to engage in this work, it will be important for studies on Native educational leadership programs that are tribally and community focused to understand the impact of incorporating tribal and Indigenous pedagogies into leadership development practices. It will also be important to document the ways in which these programs are demonstrating accountability to the communities they are serving. This documented impact will go a long way in helping to secure financial and philosophical support of these initiatives.

Recommendations for Policy and Practice

As previously discussed, Native-focused leadership programs began in earnest in the 1970s with the support of federal funding aimed at increasing the overall number and quality of American Indian and Alaska Native school leaders. The intent of this funding was to seed these programs, with the goal of colleges and universities incorporating these programs into their core operations and functions. Unfortunately, many of these programs continue to rely on federal funding because colleges and universities have not taken up the goal to authentically serve the needs of Native students, their schools, or communities. This important issue must be addressed if these programs are to move beyond basic subsistence.

As colleges and universities work to make educational leadership programs more culturally relevant for Native students, they must also work to recruit more students into these programs. Wright (1991) cited exponential increases in the number of American Indian college students between 1965 and the 1980s—increasing from 7,000 to more than 90,000. These increases can be attributed in large part to the War on Poverty, increased self-determination on the part of Native peoples, passage of laws such as the Indian Self-Determination and Education Assistance Act and The Tribally Controlled Community College Assistance Act of 1978, and movement toward increased local control of Indian education. Unfortunately, the proportion of Native college students has not maintained this pattern of significant increase over time, with Native students making up less than 1% of postsecondary enrollment today (U.S. Department of Education, National Center for Education Statistics, 2015). To increase the recruitment and retention of Native students in higher education, it is imperative that colleges and universities collaborate with tribal peoples and communities to identify potential students and to make colleges and universities academically and culturally supportive and affirming. As Austin (2005) argues, "If institutions of higher education want to improve their American Indian retention and graduation rates, they must include American Indian views and expectations in their planning. To date, however, these institutions have expressed little interest in knowing the views of tribal leaders and the parents of their American Indian students" (p. 41).

Once Native students complete their academic degree programs, efforts must also be made to ensure they are recruited and retained in leadership positions at the elementary, secondary, and postsecondary levels. Unfortunately, many Native students find themselves unable to secure leadership positions in their own tribal communities after graduation. This situation is related, in part, to the community's sense that mainstream institutions have not adequately prepared these individuals to retain their Native cultures and identities and thus to lead effectively in Native schools and communities. This speaks to the need to re-vision leadership preparation programs so that they are more readily able to embrace the role of Indigenous knowledges and ways of doing and thinking in the design and delivery of the curriculum of these programs (Battiste, 2002; Dimmock & Walker, 1998). This work must be done in collaboration with tribes and tribal organizations.

It is also important to consider recently established and evolving Native educational leadership programs that are P–20 focused to understand the impact they are having on policy and practice. This approach includes listening to the voices of tribal community leaders and educators and recognizing that our educational journeys do not end with high school graduation. Having Native educational leaders at both the K–12 and higher education levels has made important impacts on policy and practice and in our ability to effectively advocate for increased support of Indigenous education at the local, state, and national levels. In the future, it will be important for state, tribal, federal, and national organizations to connect with Native educational leadership programs to leverage their respective resources to more effectively advocate on behalf of Native American students at all levels. Connecting the currently existing K–12 Native educational leadership programs with emerging P–20-focused Native educational leadership programs is essential to advancing effective practices that impact future generations of leaders within K–12 schools, colleges and universities, and tribal communities.

Recommendations for Tribal Communities/Schools/Colleges/Citizens

Local tribal colleges and NNCUs must understand their role in creating culturally relevant and tribally based Native educational leadership programs. As we prepare to train the next generation of Native educational leaders, it will be imperative for leadership preparation programs to work in collaboration with tribes and tribal communities to ensure that aspiring leaders are well versed in the linguistic and cultural practices and traditions of the students and schools with whom they will work. This will require intensive internship- and practicum-based field experiences in these schools, colleges, and communities. It will also be critical for these leaders to espouse Indigenous values and principles of relationship, respect, and reciprocity (Kirkness & Barnhardt, 1991). Without these values, students and their families will find it difficult, if not impossible, to fully trust and engage with these new leaders.

It is also important to establish consistent collaboration and communication within these evolving Native educational leadership programs. Such communication will enable these programs to better meet the needs of the participants as well as the communities, schools, and organizations they are designed to serve. A need consistently expressed in traditional leadership preparation programs is participants' desire to remain in and/or return to their home communities upon completion of their degree program. Programs that allow tribal members who are participants of these programs to remain in their home communities promote continuous connection to their communities. One way to approach this is by offering distance education programs, by which the bulk of instruction is delivered online or via other electronic modes of communication (Austin, 2005).

Finally, it is important to identify and respond to specific gaps that exist within Native leadership in both K–12 and higher education. Colleges and universities have a responsibility to assist in filling leadership gaps within tribal schools, TCUs, and NNCUs. Tribal colleges can and should be encouraged to engage in partnerships and collaborative endeavors with NNCUs in the design and delivery of Native leadership preparation programs (Austin, 2005). It is also important to acknowledge that "the responsibility for improving leadership training in any professional field should not rest entirely with university professors. . . . Practicing administrators must have opportunities to influence the direction of program change" (Farquhar & Martin, 1972, p. 30). Failure to incorporate the professional wisdom of those who have been in the field will not serve us well as we continue to increase the number and quality of Native educational leaders.

Conclusion

Although the events of the 1960s and 1970s helped to increase the number of American Indian educational leaders, anecdotal data indicate this need persists today (Battle, 2009). Data from the 2007–2008 school year indicated that fewer than 2% of all public school principals were American Indian/Alaska Native (Battle, 2009). As more tribally controlled educational institutions emerge, and as opportunities for leadership positions within NNCUs emerge, there is an increasing need to expand the cadre of American Indian and Alaska Native educational leaders qualified to fill these positions. Unfortunately, the future of Indigenous-focused leadership programs is questionable if such programs are forced to continue to rely on funding from the federal government, with limited or no real financial support from their host institutions. Although the federal government has and should be held to its trust responsibility for Indigenous peoples, the goal of federal funding has and most likely always will be to develop administrator training programs, not to sustain them. If these programs are to flourish, they must become integral parts of the day-to-day operations of the colleges and universities within which they operate. Having said this, the caution here is that these programs must resist being subsumed by dominant Westernized approaches to leadership preparation. This is certainly a challenge, but one that can and must be undertaken if we are to enact the principles of local, tribal control and self-determination that were so ardently fought for in the 1960s and 1970s.

The successful preparation of Indigenous educational leaders requires those providing leadership development to embrace the fact that leadership preparation programs for aspiring Indigenous educational leaders must be contextually, culturally, and linguistically relevant. As Johnson, Benham, and VanAlstine (2003) so aptly write, "There is no one model of [N]ative leadership, just as every basket has its own peculiar warp and weave, each reflecting the history, culture, and language of a community of people" (p. 158).

Note

1. See www.niea.org for additional information.

References

Austin, R. D. (2005, Spring). Perspectives of American Indian nation parents and leaders. In M. J. Tippeconnic Fox, S. C. Lowe, & G. S. McClellan (Eds.), *New Directions for Student Services*, 109, 41–48.

Battiste, M. (2002). *Indigenous knowledge and pedagogy in First Nations education: A literature review with recommendations*. Ottawa: Apamuwek Institute. Retrieved from http://educationactiontoronto.com/file_download/85/4Marie-Battisteikp_e(2).pdf

Battle, D. (2009). *Characteristics of public, private, and Bureau of Indian Education elementary and secondary school principals in the United States: Results from the 2007–08 Schools and Staffing Survey* (NCES 2009-323). Washington DC: National Center for Education Statistics, Institute of Education Sciences, U.S. Department of Education.

Christman, D., Guillory, R., Fairbanks, A., & Gonzalez, M. L. (2008). A model of American Indian school administrators: Completing the circle of knowledge in Native schools. *Journal of American Indian Education, 47*(3), 53–72.

Crosby, B. C., & Bryson, J. M. (2005). *Leadership for common good: Talking public problems in a shared-power world.* New York, NY: John Wiley & Sons.

Dimmock, C., & Walker, C. (1998). Comparative educational administration: Developing a cross-cultural conceptual framework. *Educational Administration Quarterly, 34*(4), 558–595.

Faircloth, S. C., & Tippeconnic III, J. W. (2013, August). Leadership in Indigenous education: Challenges and opportunities for change. *American Journal of Education, 119*(4), 481–486.

Faircloth, S. C., & Tippeconnic III, J. W. (2015, Spring). Leadership development for schools serving American Indian students: Implications for research, policy, and practice. *Journal of American Indian Education, 54*(1), 127–153.

Farquhar, R. H., & Martin, W. (1972, September). New developments in the preparation of educational leaders. *The Phi Delta Kappan, 54*(1), 26–30.

Henderson, D., Carjuzaa, J., & Ruff, W. G. (2015). Reconciling leadership paradigms: Authenticity as practiced by American Indian school leaders. *International Journal of Multicultural Education, 17*(1), 231.

Institute for Government Research. (1928). *The problem of Indian administration* (Report of a survey made at the request of Honorable Hubert Work, Secretary of the Interior, and submitted to him, February 21, 1928). Baltimore, MD: Johns Hopkins.

Johnson, V., Benham, M. K. P., & VanAlstine, M. J. (2003). Native leadership: Advocacy for transformation, culture, community and sovereignty. In M. K. P. Benham & W. Stein (Eds.), *The renaissance of American Indian Higher Education: Capturing the dream* (pp. 149–166). Mahwah, NJ: Lawrence Erlbaum Associates.

Johnson, V. J. (1997). Weavers of change: Portraits of Native American women educational leaders. *Dissertation Abstracts International, 59*(1), 36A.

Kirkness, V. J., & Barnhardt, R. (1991). The four r's: Respect, relevance, reciprocity, responsibility. *Journal of American Indian Education, 30*(3), 1–15.

Leitka, E., Morton, R. C. B., Thompson, M., Sockey, C.E., Benham, W.J., Hopkins, T.R., Hall, R.E. (1975, April). *Evaluation report of Indian education administrator training programs at university of Harvard, Penn State ad Minnesota.* Research and Evaluation Report Series No. 22.02. Albuquerque, NM: Bureau of Indian Affairs, Department of Interior.

León, D. J., & Nevarez, C. (2007). Models of leadership institutes for increasing the number of top Latino administrators in higher education. *Journal of Hispanic Higher Education, 6*(4), 356–377.

Lomawaima, K. T., & McCarty, T. L. (2002). When tribal sovereignty challenges democracy: American Indian education and the democratic ideal. *American Educational Research Journal, 39*(2), 279–305.

Lynch, P. D. (1973). *Multi-cultural administrator training and cultural change.* Retrieved from http://files.eric.ed.gov/fulltext/ED075899.pdf

Merisotis, J. M. (2005, August). *Leading the way: Training higher education leaders through the Kellogg MSI leadership fellows program.* OECD conference on Trends in the Management of Human Resources in Higher Education Paris. Retrieved from www.oecd.org/edu/imhe/35327289.pdf

Mills, E., & Amiotte, L. (1996). American Indian Administrator Preparation: A program analysis. *Tribal College, 7*(3), 27.

National Advisory Council on Indian Education. (1975, March). *Through education: Self determination: A bicentennial goal for American Indians.* The Second Annual Report to the Congress of the United States. Washington, DC: National Advisory Council on Indian Education. ERIC Document Reproduction Service No. ED 107 438.

Oppelt, N. T. (1990). *The tribally controlled Indian colleges: The beginnings of self determination in American Indian education.* Tsaile, AZ: Navajo Community College Press. ERIC Document Reproduction Service No. ED 356 108.

Perna, L. W., & Titus, M. A. (2005, September/October). The relationship between parental involvement as social capital and college enrollment: An examination of racial/ethnic group differences. *Journal of Higher Education, 76*(5), 485–518.

Pidgeon, M. (2012). Transformation and Indigenous interconnections. In C. Kenny & T. N. Fraser (Eds.), *Living Indigenous leadership: Native narratives on building strong communities* (pp. 136–149). Vancouver, British Columbia, Canada: UBC Press.

Prucha, F.P. (1984). *The great father: The United States government and the American Indians.* Lincoln: University of Nebraska Press.

Reyhner, J. (2006). American Indian/Alaska Native Education: An overview (Update of 1994 *Phi Delta Kappa* fastback #367). Retrieved from http://jan.ucc.nau .edu/~jar/AIE/Ind_Ed.html

Snipp, C. M. (2014). American Indian education. In F. Trovato & A. Romaniuk (Eds.), *Aboriginal populations: Social, demographic, and epidemiological perspectives* (pp. 351–380). Edmonton, Alberta, Canada: University of Alberta Press.

Stein, W. J. (1999). Tribal colleges: 1968–1998. In K. G. Swisher & J. W. Tippeconnic (Eds.), *Next steps: Research and practice to advance Indian Education* (pp. 259–270). Charleston, WV: ERIC Clearinghouse on Rural Education and Small Schools.

Szasz, M. (1999). *Education and the American Indian: The road to self-determination since 1928.* Albuquerque, NM: University of New Mexico Press.

University of Arizona. (2014). *AIS graduate certificate in higher education.* Retrieved from http://ais.arizona.edu/content/ais-graduate-certificate-higher-education

U.S. Department of Education, National Center for Education Statistics. (2015). Characteristics of postsecondary faculty. *The condition of education 2015* (NCES

2015-144). Washington DC: Author. Retrieved from https://nces.ed.gov/pubs2017/2017144.pdf

Warner, L. S., & Gipp, G. E. (Eds.). (2009). *Tradition and culture in the millennium: Tribal colleges and universities.* Charlotte, NC: Information Age.

Warner, L. S., & Grint, K. (2006). American Indian ways of leading and knowing. *Leadership, 2,* 225–244.

Wright, B. (1991). *American Indian and Alaska Native higher education: Toward a new century of academic achievement and cultural integrity* (ED343771). Washington DC: Department of Education. (RC 018 630). Retrieved from http://files.eric.ed.gov/fulltext/ED343771.pdf

Wright, B., & Tierney, W. G. (1991, March). American Indians in higher education: A history of cultural conflict. *Change, 23*(2), 11–18.

8

AMERICAN INDIAN STUDENTS AND ABILITY STATUS

Considerations for Improving the College Experience[1]

John L. Garland (Choctaw)

Information, research, and data on American Indian students with disabilities are limited, especially when considering the context of higher education. The purpose of this chapter is to explore the intersection of American Indian students and disability as an introduction to deeper awareness for improving the college experience. Although higher education practice has become more informed over the past decade by research around the broad aspects of disability (Kochhar-Bryant, Bassett, & Webb, 2009; Thompson, 2012), literature gaps remain when considering American Indian students. As with most topics involving American Indian students, it is important to recognize the depth and breadth of within-group diversity among American Indian communities. Therefore, I encourage the reader to make use of this chapter as a starting point for deeper understanding of American Indian students with disabilities while adding regional, tribal, and individual experiences where necessary for constructing what it means to be an American Indian student with a disability.

American Indian students are often described as resilient, involved, successful, and persistent, yet they remain among the least likely of all racial/ethnic groups in the United States to attend and complete college (Horn & Nevill, 2006; Pavel, 1999). For those who enroll in college, American Indians are the least likely to experience collegiate success (Garland, 2010a; Horn & Nevill, 2006; Tierney, 1992) and are proportionally the most likely to report having a disability (Garland, 2010a). College students with disabilities are increasingly finding opportunities for college access due to the increased competence of helping and education professionals, assistive technologies, high-school-to-college transition programs, web-based academic opportunities, and the destigmatization of disability in U.S. society (Council for the Advancement of Standards, 2012; Goff & Higbee, 2008; Oslund, 2014). Likewise, higher education professionals are increasingly playing an important role in collegiate success for students with disabilities as they gain new evidence-based practices to improve student outcomes (Kochhar-Bryant et al., 2009). However, among data on college student outcomes, American Indian students are rarely discussed in research findings, thereby limiting our understanding of American Indian college students in general, and especially those with disabilities (Garland, 2010a). Although progress has been made in recent years specific to research outcomes focusing on American Indian college students (Shotton, Lowe, & Waterman, 2013), the intersections of specific variables such as disability and race remain less explored.

Finding and reviewing data on American Indian college students with disabilities becomes complicated when data collected at institutional and national levels are reported among other racial/ethnic groups. When such data are reported collectively, American Indian representation is often statistically powerless, resulting in invisibility among quantitative research findings. This is especially true for American Indian data related to students with disabilities (Garland, 2010b). This phenomenon of quantitative data invisibility is referred to as the "American Indian research asterisk" (Garland, 2007, p. 612).

The Problem With Overgeneralization and Within-Group Differences

Overgeneralizing research on specific racial and ethnic groups to individual members can become a barrier to deeper understanding. For example, when considering American Indian college students and the limited research/data available to higher education professionals, overgeneralization of existing research and data across all American Indian students is convenient but not advisable. The more than 500 Indigenous tribes in the United States and its colonial territories, many of whom may speak unique languages, present a simple illustration of the wide within-group differences often not discussed in research or accounted for in data collected on race/ethnicity. Some researchers have begun to collect specific tribal affiliations when collecting data by race, but they need to collapse American Indian tribal data back into a single group to increase an already low-power statistic in comparison with other racial groups.

If one were to ask Natives and non-Natives in the United States how they construct Native American identity, one is likely to get as many different answers as people asked. However, American Indians in the United States share many common experiences related to colonialism, historical trauma, and racism. Societal stereotypes continue to prevail about American Indians, such as that most live on land reserves (reservations), all Natives receive free college education, or we all share the same phenotype (physical characteristics such as skin color and features) (Mihesuah, 1996), when in reality broad variations of within-group differences are widely evident, even within a single tribe. That being said, generalized data findings may be helpful as a first step to identifying evidence-based needs and resource allocations in higher education. As next steps, however, researchers may need to focus on non-quantitative methods for appreciating specific within-group differences by tribe, campus Native population(s), region, and other variables. In doing so, higher education professionals may design educational interventions specific to their campus, region, and/or tribal needs. It is also important to acknowledge that each tribe and individual tribal member may construct disability, and what it means to have a disability, differently than others. As such, the broad research and data discussed in this chapter provide the reader with a starting point for engaging the intersecting paths of American Indian students and disability from the perspectives of campus and community.

A recent example of a particular within-group difference as it indirectly relates to Native students was reported by Lombardi, Murray, and Gerdes (2012). They found significant variance among first-generation college students with and without a disability. Specifically, they found that, among students with disabilities, first-generation students reported lower GPAs, less available family support, lower peer support, and greater financial stress than their non-first-generation counterparts (Lombardi et al., 2012). From an intersectional perspective, these data are important because we know American Indian students are overrepresented among those who are also first-generation college students (Horn & Nevill, 2006).

Overview of Disability in College

Houtenville, Stapleton, Weathers, and Burkhauser (2009) reported a significant rise in the number of individuals with disabilities seeking a college education. For 2007–2008, that percentage was nearly 10%. A 2009 National Center for Education Statistics (NCES) report (Snyder, Dillow, & Hoffman, 2009) found that at least 6% of all college students identified with a disability. Across undergraduate settings in colleges and universities, the NCES report for 2011–2012 (Snyder & Dillow, 2015) found that percentage increased to at least 11% of college students. Within the 2009 group, 46% reported having a learning disability, 14% reported an orthopedic or a mobility impairment, 8% reported mental illness or an emotional disability, 6% reported being deaf or hard of hearing, 4% reported visual impairments, and 9% reported having a speech impairment (Snyder et al., 2009). In 2008–2009, students with disabilities were enrolled in almost every 2- and 4-year institution in the United States (Raue & Lewis, 2011). With the increased accessibility of physical and virtual environments and new advances in technology, we should anticipate that more students with disabilities will be seeking access to higher education environments. Additionally, advances in medicine and rehabilitation techniques are resulting in greater opportunities for people to survive traumatic accidents and difficult births. Improvements in technology are also making it possible for more people with disabilities to live independently, whereas as recently as a decade ago, those same individuals may have been dependent on others for basic care. Federal and state mandates for precollege academic support programs are helping more students with disabilities complete high school, thereby opening opportunities for postsecondary education. The broadening public awareness of legislation and accommodations, coupled with less stigma associated with disabilities, is creating a more inclusive and equitable educational environment for students with disabilities (Garland, 2015).

College students who share a similar disability may also have varying approaches when it comes to achieving specific tasks in the learning environment. Therefore, campus accommodations should vary from student to student even when students have the same disability. Ultimately, a student who has a disability requires accommodations only when a task requires a skill that the current environment precludes. For example, if a student informs a campus staff member of his or her disability and would like to explore accommodations, the staff member should involve the student in developing strategies to eliminate or minimize barriers rather than imposing a prescriptive solution. Students are often the best source of information for designing accommodations for their particular disability (Oslund, 2014), so campus staff and administrators should be open to creative solutions that fully involve the student (Garland, 2015; Thompson, 2012). The following concepts, terms, and perspectives are important tools for creating informed, positive, and effective campus environments for Native students with disabilities.

Tribal Constructions of Disability

It is important to recognize that constructions of disability may vary across tribal affiliation and may even differ within a tribe, especially if the tribe is spread across a large geographical area that may be divided by international, state, cultural, and/or geographical boundaries. Varying perspectives of self in relation to social, natural, and spiritual balance may result in a disability identity that is focused on one's relationship with the natural world rather than a focus on self with a disability (Lovern, 2008). Tribes with vocational rehabilitation and disability services may have formal relationships with government-sponsored disability services resulting in resources tailored to those relationship guidelines. For example, relationships with state government vocational rehabilitation services are unique to each state and may vary from state to state. Likewise, the Indian Health Service may provide its own criteria for disability services to its consumers that may differ from individual tribal services. Therefore, it is important for campus disability services personnel to be aware of these potential differences when working with Native students with disabilities.

Federal Legislation

Section 504 of the Rehabilitation Act of 1973 and the Americans with Disabilities Act of 1990 prohibit discrimination against individuals with disabilities. According to these laws, "No otherwise qualified person with a disability shall, solely by reason of disability, be excluded from the participation in, be denied the benefits of, or be subjected to discrimination under any program or activity of a public entity." This means that college and university services and information, as well as academic offerings, must be accessible to otherwise qualified students with disabilities.

Students Who Qualify for Disability Services ("Otherwise Qualified")

"Otherwise qualified," with respect to postsecondary educational services, refers to a student who meets the academic and technical standards required for admission or participation in the campus program or activity with or without reasonable modification to rules, policies, or practices; the removal of architectural, communication, or transportation barriers; or the provision of auxiliary aids and services. Campus disability services staff members are trained to help their campuses comply with this part of the Rehabilitation Act of 1973.

Disability

Disability is, of course, a social construct. Disability advocates argue that, although a person may have a disability, environmental and societal barriers often keep a person with a disability from fully engaging his or her learning environment. Consequently, campus disability services focus on removing, accommodating, and/or navigating barriers (physical, psychological, virtual, etc.) so that optimum campus engagement is possible (Council for the Advancement of Standards, 2012). Disabilities covered by legislation include but are not limited to spinal cord injuries, loss of limbs, multiple sclerosis, muscular dystrophy, cerebral palsy, hearing impairments, speech impairments, specific learning disabilities, head injuries (including concussion), mental health disorders (including attention-deficit/hyperactive disorder [ADHD]), diabetes, cancer, immune deficiencies, and others. Disabilities are not always readily apparent to campus administrators, and therefore we should avoid making any assumptions regarding a student's disability status based on visual presentation. The campus disability services coordinator is typically responsible for documenting and coordinating verification of a student's disability (Garland, 2015).

Transition

Many legal, policy, and advocacy aspects affecting the experiences of students with disabilities in secondary education exist. Federal and state education legislation shapes how students learn and progress within secondary education settings. Once a student completes secondary education, the process for accessing and advocating for disability resources in higher education generally becomes the responsibility of the student or the student's legal guardian. This change from a paternalistic approach to one of self-advocacy may be challenging for new college students with disabilities, and support measures should be in place for students who may have difficulty adjusting (Garland, 2015). If a student was receiving disability support services prior to college, the student was likely using what is called an Individualized Education Plan (IEP) to guide high school disability support services. A component of the IEP provides for transition planning to vocational training, supported work environments, and higher education. For students with an IEP who are planning to transition to higher education, the IEP may include access plans and training for resources such as college preparation assessments, transportation needs assessments, and psychological evaluations. Each plan will be specific to a student's individual needs. The level and quality of college transition services may vary from state to state, but campus disability professionals are trained to help students who had an IEP prior to college transition to higher education.

Data on American Indians With Disabilities

What we do know at this time is that among people ages 21 to 64 years, disabilities are more prevalent among Native Americans (22.5%) than all other racial/ethnic groups (Snyder et al., 2009). For example, 17% of Blacks reported having a disability, followed by Whites at 12.6%, Hispanic/Latino community members 10.7%, and Asian Americans at 6.3% (Horn & Nevill, 2006). Researchers have found that bachelor's degree attainment for working-age people with disabilities is 12.5%, students with disabilities are more likely to enroll at 2-year and vocational training colleges (32%) than 4-year colleges (25%) (Houtenville et al., 2009), and public colleges and universities are more likely to enroll students with disabilities than private institutions (Horn & Nevill, 2006; Houtenville et al., 2009).

Although Houtenville and colleagues (2009) found that 6% of all undergraduates self-report having a disability, a secondary analysis of a national data set (Garland, 2010b) found that 22.1% of American Indian students enrolled in college reported having a disability. From this study, American Indian college students attending primarily four-year non-Native colleges and universities self-reported the following apparent and nonapparent disabilities: learning, visual, hearing, physical, psychiatric, ADHD, neurologic, and/or medical (e.g., asthma, diabetes) (Garland, 2010a). Collectively, these data create a complicated picture of the American Indian college student experience and indicate the need for further exploration.

In a recent national study (Garland, 2010a) that included 1,959 American Indian college student respondents comprising 2.07% of the study's sample across all races, roughly 1 in 5 reported having a disability (22.1%), which is consistent with national data. Within the American Indian data, 33% identified as male, 23% were first generation, and 93% were considered full time. Medical disabilities (e.g., asthma, diabetes) constituted the largest percentage (39%) of those reporting a disability, including those with multiple disabilities (Garland, 2010b). The category of psychiatric and/or psychological disability was the second highest self-reported category, with 37% of the American Indian respondents reporting. This category was followed by ADHD (22%), learning disability (17%), physical disability (13%), hearing/visual impairment (10% each), and speech/language disability at 5% (Garland, 2010a). Although these data were originally analyzed to explore outcomes of American Indian student involvement in the collegiate environment, they provide us with rare insight for American Indian students with disabilities from a national sample. Again, for comparison, the NCES reports that roughly 6% of all undergraduates report having a disability: 29% learning, 23% orthopedic (e.g., physical), 21% "other" health-related disability, 16% hearing, 15% visual, and 3% speech (Horn & Nevill, 2006). These data are helpful, but they only provide a broad view with few details, thus indicating a greater need for tribal and individual Native student experience data. In the next section, I identify implications for practice in higher education and considerations for future research.

Implications for Practice

Students with disabilities transition through several environments: from a K–12-driven system to postsecondary environments that rely on students to self-advocate (Johnson, Sharpe, & Stodden, 2000). For more in-depth reading on transition, Kochhar-Bryant and colleagues (2009) have an excellent book on understanding the postsecondary transition process for students with disabilities. I also suggest the following:

1. Identify and reach out to American Indian students directly and build relationships with local Native American communities and family systems.
2. Publicize disability support services to American Indian student groups/organizations, local Native communities, and tribes.
3. Be inclusive of American Indian students when talking about racial/ethnic groupings across disability.
4. Understand that American Indian college student populations may be comprised of broad within-group diversity (tribal, regional, etc.) and may approach having a disability differently from one another.

Future Considerations for Research

Conduct/identify new studies that include:

- American Indians with disabilities reporting success measures in college (e.g., GPA/graduation);
- American Indians with disabilities reporting cognitive development in college;
- American Indians with disabilities reporting career-related college outcomes;
- specific accommodation needs for American Indian college students with disabilities; and
- transition services from high school to college for American Indian college students with disability.

People-First Language

The Centers for Disease Control and Prevention (CDC) (Hootman, Brault, Helmick, Theis, & Armour, 2014) estimates that as many as 50 million Americans report having a disability. More important, the CDC states that most Americans will experience a disability at some point during the course of their lives. Disability is presented in varying and unique forms relative to the individual. Higher education environments are increasingly focused on aspects of social justice, inclusion, and equity. A critical component of this movement is respect for the individual. Nowhere is this more important than when working with people with disabilities. People-first language, sometimes referred to as person-first language, emphasizes the person, not the disability. The CDC provides the following language suggestions for communicating with and about people with disabilities (see Table 8.1). Visit www.cdc.gov/ncbddd/disabilityandhealth for the full downloadable list.

TABLE 8.1
Examples of People-First Language

People-First Language	Language to Avoid
Person with a disability	The disabled, handicapped
Person without a disability	Normal person, healthy person
Person with an intellectual, cognitive, or developmental disability	Insane, crazy, psycho, maniac, nuts
Person who is hard of hearing	Hearing impaired, suffers a hearing loss
Person who is deaf	Deaf and dumb, mute
Person who is blind	Visually impaired, the blind
Person who has a communication disorder, is unable to speak, or uses a device to speak	Mute, dumb
Person who uses a wheelchair	Confined or restricted to a wheelchair, wheelchair-bound
Person with a physical disability, physically disabled	Crippled, lame, deformed, invalid, spastic
Person with autism	Autistic
Person with epilepsy or seizure disorder	Epileptic
Person with multiple sclerosis	Afflicted by multiple sclerosis
Person with cerebral palsy	Cerebral palsy victim
Accessible parking or bathroom	Handicapped parking or bathroom
Person of short stature	Midget
Person with a congenital disability	Birth defect
Person with Down syndrome	Mongoloid
Person who is successful and productive	Has overcome disability, is courageous

Of course, each student with a disability may have personal preference(s) when referring to a particular disability, but this list is a place to begin. Although popular culture does not generally practice people-first language, one should attempt (without shaming self or others when unsure) to be as inclusive as possible when communicating with others (Garland, 2015). With regard to Indigenous identity, individuals and tribes prefer different terminology; therefore, it is always best to ask how an individual wishes to be identified.

Conclusion

The information reported in this chapter includes data that are critical to advancing knowledge and understanding about American Indian college students with disabilities. Overall, the types of disabilities reported by Native students are consistent with those among overall student disability statistics. However, Native students are at least three times as likely to report a disability as non-Native students. By deepening our understanding of American Indian college students with disabilities through more research and data, we will be better able to design transition and support programs for enhancing Native student success. The following is a list of resources to access.

Higher Education Disability Resources

American College Personnel Association (ACPA) Standing Committee on Disability, One Dupont Circle NW, Suite 300, Washington DC 20036. (202) 835-2272. www.acpa.nche.edu

Association on Higher Education and Disability (AHEAD): AHEAD Professional Standards. www.ahead.org

Consortia of Administrators for Native American Rehabilitation (CANAR). www.canar.org

Council for the Advancement of Standards (CAS): CAS Standards— Disability Support Services. www.cas.edu

National Center for Universal Design for Learning. www.udlcenter.org

Universal Design: North Carolina State University Center for Universal Design. www.ncsu.edu/project/design-projects/udi/center-for-universal-design/

University of Washington DO-IT (Disabilities, Opportunities, Internetworking, and Technology) Center. www.washington.edu/doit/

Note

1. This chapter was supported, in part, by a grant from the NASPA Foundation.

References

Council for the Advancement of Standards. (2012). *CAS professional standards for higher education* (8th edition). Washington, DC: Author.

Garland, J. L. (2007). Review of the book *Serving Native American students: New directions for student services*. *Journal of College Student Development, 48,* 612–614.

Garland, J. L. (2010a). *Removing the college involvement "research asterisk": Identifying and rethinking predictors of American Indian college student involvement.* Retrieved from Dissertations & Theses: Full Text. (Publication No. AAT 3426253).

Garland, J. L. (2010b, October). American Indian students with disabilities: New data from a national study. Paper presented at the National Rehabilitation Association annual training conference, New Orleans, LA.

Garland, J. L. (2015). Commuter students with disabilities. In J. P. Biddix (Ed.), *Understanding and addressing commuter student needs* (pp. 57–67). San Francisco, CA: Jossey-Bass.

Goff, E., & Higbee, J. L. (Eds.). (2008). *Pedagogy and student services for institutional transformation: Implementation guidebook for faculty and instructional staff.* Minneapolis: University of Minnesota, College of Education and Human Development.

Hootman, J. M., Brault, M. W., Helmick, C. G., Theis, K. A., & Armour, B. S. (2014). Prevalence and most common causes of disability among adults—United States, 2005. *MMWR Morb Mortal Wkly Rep, 58*(16), 421–426.

Horn, L., & Nevill, S. (2006). *Profile of undergraduates in U.S. postsecondary education institutions, 2003–04: With a special analysis of community college students* (NCES 2006-184). Washington DC: U.S. Department of Education, National Center for Education Statistics.

Houtenville, A. J., Stapleton, D. C., Weathers, R. R., & Burkhauser, R. V. (Eds.). (2009). *Counting working-age people with disabilities: What current data tell us and options for improvement.* Kalamazoo, MI: W. E. Upjohn Institute for Employment Research.

Johnson, D. R., Sharpe, M., & Stodden, R. (2000). The transition to postsecondary education for students with disabilities. *IMPACT, 13*(1), 2–3.

Kochhar-Bryant, C., Bassett, D. S., & Webb, K. W. (2009). *Transition to postsecondary education for students with disabilities.* Thousand Oaks, CA: SAGE Publications.

Lombardi, A. R., Murray, C., & Gerdes, H. (2012). Academic performance of first-generation college students with disabilities. *Journal of College Student Development, 53*(6), 811–826.

Lovern, L. (2008). Native American worldview and the discourse on disability. *Essays in Philosophy, 1*(9).

Mihesuah, D. A. (1996). *American Indians: Stereotypes and realities.* Atlanta, GA: Clarity Press, Inc.

Oslund, C. (2014). *Supporting college and university students with invisible disabilities.* Philadelphia, PA: Jessica Kingsley Publishers.

Pavel, D. M. (1999). American Indians and Alaska Natives in higher education. In K. Swisher & J. Tippeconnic (Eds.), *Next steps: Research and practice to advance Indian education* (pp. 193–214). Charleston, WV: ERIC Clearinghouse on Rural Education and Small Schools.

Raue, K., & Lewis, L. (2011). *Students with disabilities at degree-granting postsecondary institutions* (NCES 2011-018). U.S. Department of Education, National Center for Education Statistics. Washington DC: Government Printing Office.

Shotton, H. J., Lowe, S. C., & Waterman, S. J. (Eds.). (2013). *Beyond the asterisk: Understanding native students in higher education.* Sterling, VA: Stylus.

Snyder, T. D., & Dillow, S. A. (2015). *Digest of education statistics, 2013* (NCES 2015-011). Washington DC: National Center for Education Statistics, Institute of Education Sciences, U.S. Department of Education.

Snyder, T. D., Dillow, S. A., & Hoffman, C. M. (2009). *Digest of Education Statistics 2008* (NCES 2009-020). Washington DC: National Center for Education Statistics, Institute of Education Sciences, U.S. Department of Education.

Thompson, M. V. (2012). Expanding the frame: Applying universal design in higher education, Part I. *Developments, 10*(1).

Tierney, W.G. (1992). *Official encouragement, institutional discouragement: Minorities in academe: The Native American experience.* Norwood, NJ: Ablex.

CONCLUSION
Achieving the ~~Im~~Possible
Stephanie J. Waterman (Onondaga), Shelly C. Lowe (Diné),
Heather J. Shotton, (Wichita/Kiowa/Cheyenne), and Jerry Bread (Kiowa/Cherokee)

> Exploring the impact of college-prep programs on Native students' transitions and success in college would offer insight into the program characteristics that promote access and attainment. Researchers should also never underestimate the power of Native students' stories of struggle and success. Through these stories, students elaborate on the knowledge and experiences that helped them realize their potential to persevere. (Youngbull, chapter 1, p. 29)

As Youngbull so aptly wrote in chapter 1, this book reflects the importance of Indigeneity in developing, maintaining, and supporting college access programs. Youngbull is an example of a successful Native graduate who can pinpoint that success to her being exposed to the idea of attending college through the Colorado University Upward Bound (CUUB) program, a program uniquely designed for Indigenous students. Her ability to navigate undergraduate and graduate school was impacted by a number of programs specifically meant to increase the success of Native students. In addition to Youngbull's story, Breanna, Monty, Nakay, and Corey shared their stories of navigating higher education as Indigenous students. Each of these students has his or her own journey accessing higher education, and each has been supported by various entities. Family, Native faculty and staff support, a supportive campus community or an LGBTQ group, along with programs that offer funding, such as the McNair Scholars and Gates Millennium Scholars Program, were instrumental to their access.

Breanna's success began with a guidance counselor who made sure she applied for the Gates Scholarship, like her sister who was a Gates Scholarship recipient. She also had support from her high school friends who made sure she had rides to school. Corey was also a Gates Scholarship recipient and acknowledged that Native faculty mentors were critical to his educational journey. In addition to participating in a summer bridge program before entering college, he also benefited from Native role models during his undergraduate years when exposure to social justice helped him change his educational goals.

151

Nakay lacked family support but was able to make a family and find support within an Indigenous LGBTQ community. After an Indigenous graduate student reached out to offer help applying to graduate programs, Nakay ended up attending Harvard University and connecting with on-campus support systems. These doctoral students' experiences directly challenge the stereotypes expressed by non-Natives in the opening of this book. Their stories demonstrate that Native students do go to college, they can and do succeed, and, with the help of their families, Native communities, and targeted programs, they are creating pathways through postsecondary education. Monty experienced challenges gaining access to graduate education, but he was able to overcome those challenges through support and mentoring from Native faculty and higher education professionals. He developed strong support networks with other Native graduate students. Monty acknowledged the central role of his grandfather in his life and his ability to persevere.

As Monty's story illustrates, had there not been Indigenous faculty, advanced graduate students, or staff to look out for talent within our Indigenous student pool, we wonder where some of our graduate students and new doctorates would be today. CUUB (chapter 1) and College Horizons (chapter 2) have clearly had an impact in increasing access. These programs are effective because they are initiated and supported by Indigenous communities. Indigenous worldviews and role models are foundational to these programs. They are neither add-ons nor an avenue to include diversity, nor are they generic support programs tweaked for an Indigenous population. These programs are designed by us, for us. In this book, we made a concerted effort to privilege the voices of Indigenous students and recent graduates who have experienced and benefited from Indigenous-centered programs.

In this conclusion, we highlight points from the chapters and discuss the concept of Native social capital as it relates to nation-building, a concept repeated throughout the book. We then share a program designed to enhance a college culture within the Norman Public School system in Oklahoma, the College Links program, as an example of a program designed by us, for us. We close this chapter with acknowledgment of this book's limitations and a summary of recommendations.

Chapter Highlights

We first bring attention to the self-determination education timeline shared by Faircloth and Minthorn in their chapter, "The Evolution of Native Education Leadership" (chapter 7), which features legislation and federal reports that have influenced Native American educational policies and in turn have impacted college access for Native students. Some of this legislation allowed tribes to create their own formal higher education systems, further increasing access to education, whereas other legislation encouraged non-Native colleges and universities to recruit Native students into areas of study that would in return impact tribal communities on a larger scale, a trend that continues today, as seen in chapter 5 with support for science, technology, engineering, and mathematics (STEM) degree attainment. Graduates and communities that have benefited from these efforts have shown that educational attainment supports and strengthens Native nation building. Their successes have led to increasing leadership in Native student access. College Horizons is an example of such a program. Led by both Native and non-Native experts, the program provides students with the guidance and encouragement to apply to college while simultaneously offering the opportunity for students to expand their college support networks.

In her work with students in College Horizons, Keene addresses notions of identity, asking us to look beyond the traditional, reservation-raised or connected student to better understand the wide range of Native identity. Her work also broadens the concept of reciprocity—giving back as honoring those who came before and those who will come after. Although Native identity is complex, with identities ranging from traditional with a knowledge of ceremony and language, to a budding awareness and exploration, to enrolled and disenfranchised, urban, reservation, and everything in between, that knowledge, and being able to accept Indigenous students for who they are in that complexity, is important. The student voices in this book make note of the mentors whose actions encouraged their talents as Native-identified students. Indigenous mentors served as role models, read scholarship applications, volunteered as faculty for College Horizons, identified potential students and leaders, and shared their own educational pathways with students.

What makes Native mentors stand out is an understanding of Native identity. Being able to recognize that diversity without judgment is key. An Indigenous mentor can see past the prevailing non-Indigenous markers of leadership and success to identify the potential in the quiet Native student who is intuitive and knowledgeable, the one who may not have come from a well-resourced school yet shows high academic ability, and those students who will succeed because they want to give back to their communities and maintain their culture and language. Native mentors are also often more understanding of the kinds of opportunities Native graduates will consider upon degree completion. For example, Danielle Terrance (Mohawk) once shared that after she earned her master's degree and entered the job market, she noted how her classmates were engaging in national job searches, whereas she wanted to stay close to family, which limited the number of jobs for which she could apply. The need to remain close to home also limited the support she received from her institution's career services office and the encouragement she received from non-Native faculty and classmates.

Indigenized programs encourage and create pathways for graduates to return home for employment. The Recruitment and Retention of Alaska Natives into Nursing (RRANN) program is a perfect example. Although not all of the students in the program are Alaska Native, they are trained and encouraged to fill high-demand nursing positions back in their home communities or in tribal health facilities, such as the one in Anchorage, Alaska. RRANN is also an example of how the role of Indigenous knowledge systems (IKSs) and Native social capital can guide an access program through the inclusion of the Ten Universal Alaska Native Values (Alaska Native Knowledge Network, n.d.). Although RRANN was designed by a non-Native, Native social capital and IKSs were valued and respected for their importance to the success of Native students and are subsequently woven into and throughout the program.

Native Social Capital

Several chapters in this book discuss the value and presence of Native social capital. Far too often, the social capital valued in higher education is based on certain social networks that lead to individual gains and benefits. This type of capital is usually associated with the "culture," literature, media, knowledge, and habits valued by the upper, White, European class (Bourdieu, 1986). The social capital referred to in some of the student narratives in this book is simply having adequate knowledge necessary to actively engage in education, apply for college, and achieve degree attainment. For example, as previously stated, the College Horizons program instructs students on the intricacies of the college application process and introduces students to college social networks such as faculty, admissions officers, and college and university alumni. The program also teaches students how to rely on their own Native social capital. This capital can be seen in their tribe's cultural ways of knowing and being, their tribal community's encouragement for their educational success, understanding their tribe's history, and knowing the high value their tribal community places on education as a tool for Native nation building. "It is the *what* that is learned in the community" (Waterman & Lindley, 2013, p. 147).

The *what* that is learned in Native communities forms Native social capital, which in return supports our resiliency to function in non-Native environments and to continue as a people (Ward, 2005). Native values are the foundation of Native social capital. Through and with Native social capital, our students are in a position to Indigenize their college spaces by connecting their tribal values and cultural ways to their everyday college experiences (Windchief & Joseph, 2015). These values are the *what* that is being incorporated into the access programs and narratives shared in this book. Connecting a college-going culture with Native social capital relies on educators and higher education institutions to follow the community's lead because creating successful Native college going begins in the community. The next section shares an illustration of using Native social capital to create a college-going environment through a program designed by a community for Indigenous students.

Norman Public Schools Links Program

The College Links program is a higher education program in the Norman Public Schools (NPS) system for Oklahoma Indigenous students. It is designed to expose students to higher education through early and consistent college engagement in an effort to alleviate any disconnect between the students' home and school cultures. Utilizing Native cultural values to inspire students to attend college, the program works to integrate college knowledge into the public school culture. This objective is achieved through campus visits to the University of Oklahoma (OU) and surrounding area colleges, offering various workshops and career fairs to highlight college and career opportunities, and mentoring from the NPS Indian Education Program staff and OU Native faculty, staff, and students (College Links Outline, 2014). The program exposes Native students to real-life college experiences and expectations through a partnership program with the OU Native American Studies program.

Linking Home Life Culture With Higher Education Culture

The College Links program began as a collaboration between the NPS Indian Education Student Services office and Jerry Bread, who served as faculty and Outreach Coordinator for the OU Native American Studies Program. Bread initiated the Links program as a response to a request by Lucyann Harjo, the director of Indian Education Student Services, a Title VII-funded program in NPS. Harjo was looking to offer Native youth something different to supplement the traditional student support services offered in conventional Indian education programs. Drawing on his years of experience in Indian Education and higher education, as well as his work with public school and college Native student advocacy, Bread envisioned a program that would serve as an early introduction to college culture as well as a recruitment mechanism for Native students. The idea was to bring Native students to OU's campus in stages to introduce them to various aspects of college going, including familiarization with a college campus and connection to Native role models.

Bread focused his attention on the theory of "cultural discontinuity," a concept well documented in the literature, which relates to students' transition from their home culture environments to the public school/college environment. As summarized by Huffman (2001), "the major theme included in the conceptual development of cultural conflict is a notion of some discrepancy between the values, behaviors, or political/economic power of those of the dominant status and those of the minori[tized] status" (p. 2). Collective, family-oriented worldviews are often in conflict with systems of higher education, which emphasize individualism, competition, and social class movement. Many Native families are still first generation without experiential knowledge of higher education. Although the NPS culture exposes students to the higher education context, a college-going culture is encouraged through Links. Hence, the program focuses on four components: the student, the parents/family (home environment), the public school the student attends, and a four-year college/university. The goal is to "link" all four components to formulate a strong linkage to equally support the student's interests, home environment, school attending, and potential college of choice, thus the name "College Links."

Approach

Initially, the focus of College Links was on creating college awareness with elementary/middle-school Native students in NPS. The pilot program utilized an early education-extended family approach, in which faculty, staff, and students served the roles of extended family members (aunties/uncles, sisters/brothers, etc.) for participants. The program provided hands-on college awareness activities and was formulated and tested among second-, third-, seventh-, and eighth-grade students. The intent was to introduce and expose these students to the meaning and purpose of college through cultural communication trust models using college students, faculty, and community members. For example, the second and third graders were brought to campus to meet Native students who took the role of older brothers/sisters/cousins. These older siblings/cousins took the students to campus locations (e.g., library, student union, classrooms, football stadium, American Indian Student Life office, cafeteria, dormitory, gymnasium, etc.) to let them experience what it was like to be an OU student. During the visit, Native faculty visited with the students providing the role of aunties/uncles/parents/grandparents, encouraging the students to be good people and good students so they might achieve a college education and be rewarded later in life.

The program grew to include juniors and graduating seniors from the two NPS high schools. The activities for high school students moved beyond college exposure by focusing on how to navigate college admissions processes and equip themselves with the tools necessary to be successful in college. Related activities consisted of exposing high school students to the college culture through OU campus visits and "College Knowledge" sessions, where they learned about college culture, the value of a college degree, and the requirements for admission, enrollment, degree progress, and graduation. Other College Knowledge session topics included: getting ready to go to college, college jargon and networking, financial concerns (including real-life budgeting), socialization, identity and self-awareness, athletics, politics, family and community support, the role of culture, and grades in college. In an effort to extend college-going culture to the home, students were encouraged to share the information with their parents and other friends, relatives, and teachers.

Native students from OU served as hosts and conducted presentations during the public school visitations. These college students, along with faculty/staff members throughout the university setting, provided a tour of the college, followed by lunch in the main student cafeteria at the expense of the university student life center. Parents and grandparents of College Links students were also invited and encouraged to participate in activities, such as the campus visit, to also be exposed to the college information sessions. OU students were also hired as academic support personnel in the NPS Indian Education Student Service program as a result of their involvement with the College Links visitations. From all indications, the College Links program has had a meaningful impact on NPS Native students. More than 1,200 Native students, grades 2 through 12, have participated over the past 5 years. Other intervention activities have also evolved as a result of the project's activities. A sense of partnership has emerged between NPS and OU, with the beneficiaries being the broader Native community in Norman, Oklahoma. More impressive are the requests from other Oklahoma Indian Education service offices asking for guidance and support in developing and implementing similar activities like the NPS College Links program. The following are some examples of current College Links programming:

- You Can Go to College—A college visit program for second-grade students with a focus on reading, math, and science.
- Battle of the Books—A fourth-grade reading competition in 17 of NPS's elementary schools that challenges all fourth-grade Native students to read 200 books throughout the school year. The event culminates with a quiz bowl competition with questions related to the assigned books.
- Science Club—The club began in 2011 with a partnership among the NPS Indian Education Student Services, OU School of Geoscience,

and the OU American Indian Science and Engineering Society (AISES) chapter. Science Club is made up of elementary through high school Native students and meets periodically throughout the school year on OU's campus. Students are exposed to various aspects of science with a focus on the connection between science and IKS.

- Mini-Festival—In partnership with the Chickasaw Nation Arts in Education Program, this program exposes third-grade students and teachers to the history and culture of southeast Oklahoma tribes through storytelling, music, art, and language.
- Drop-Out Prevention—This program focuses on building relationships among the Indian Education Student Service program, the school, its staff, and Native American families to improve on the academic success of students through effective intervention.

The example of the College Links program emphasizes an important aspect of developing Indigenous pathways to higher education, which is the place of role models. Starting at a young age, it is important for Native students to see supportive Native role models—teachers, faculty, staff, and students— who value and participate in higher education. Indigenous students need safe environments in which to grow, especially given the complicated and painful history that many of our Indigenous families have experienced, and continue to experience, with colonized education systems. Native role models are critical to creating safe environments. As such, Native students, staff, and faculty need educational spaces safe from predators, violence, suppression, and oppression.

Limitations

The programs and approaches highlighted in this book serve as examples of what our Indigenous communities are doing to create their own pathways to higher education. Many other access programs exist; however, we were unable to feature all of them. We urge our readers to look into programs such as College Horizon and organizations such as the American Indian Science and Engineering Society (AISES) or the American Indian Graduate Center (AIGC) for more information. We also urge readers to find out what access programs are offered by or with local tribal communities in their region. We were not able to include programs specifically designed by and for Native Hawaiian or Pacific Islander communities, both of whom have strong college-going cultures and unique college access considerations. We hope this book will provide information for communities to begin their own access programs, grounded in their own cultural values, to enhance college knowledge and encourage stronger college-going communities.

Recommendations

A recommendation that stands out from each chapter is the importance of role models, particularly Native faculty and staff. Unfortunately, Native faculty, especially in the tenured ranks, make up less than 1% of the total faculty in the United States (Almanac of Higher Education, 2016). In addition, Native faculty, who most often willingly engage in supporting Native students and communities, may experience an extra "tax" on their work load that can impact their research and publication record, which in turn can impact the tenure process. It is clear that higher education institutions need to hire more Native faculty and staff, and not solely in Native-centered programs, departments, and offices, or only at lower level faculty and staff positions. Many of the programs featured in this book have made a dedicated effort to connect Native American role models, faculty, and staff to students at all levels both on and off campus to help create a college-going culture.

Another key element to building a college-going culture is communication. Tribal education departments are in a unique position to take the lead in this arena by sending out regular information via e-mails and social media. Such information could include financial aid and scholarship opportunities and deadlines, internship and summer opportunities, college exploration events, and suggested ways in which the community can support college going. Because up to 85% of Native Americans in rural areas lack access to the Internet, especially at high broadband speeds (FCC Native Nations, 2017), printed media, radio, and word of mouth also serve as adequate ways to share information. The point is intentional, proactive methods of sharing timely information to everyone is key.

To share useful and informed information on Native college going, we need data. Garland (chapter 8) noted that Native Americans are more likely to report a disability, yet because of the Native American asterisk, finding data about Native students with disability is difficult. Too many institutions do not consistently collect data that could inform and enhance Native student support and institutional effectiveness. Tribal colleges and universities (TCUs), in particular, oversee a myriad of responsibilities and more often than not do not have the capacity to staff an institutional research office. Sanders and Makomenaw (chapter 3) suggest creating more articulation agreements and collaborations with four-year institutions and urge all TCUs to participate in the National Student Clearinghouse. With the introduction of mixed- and multiple-race categories available on college admissions applications, tracking the number of Native students who are gaining access and moving through higher education has become more complicated. We acknowledge that Native identity is a paradigm, as explained by Horse (2001), made up of how one conceives of one's own identity, along with both legal and tribal recognition, as well as acceptance and connection to a community. Yet some ability to accurately track Native student access, retention, program effectiveness, and degree attainment is important, particularly for assessment and accountability.

Institutional accountability needs to start by addressing the data issue, but it also needs to include a review of appropriate and impactful funding for Native programs on campus. As pointed out in chapter 5, many STEM programs are created and funded through federal and organizational dollars. Unfortunately, when this funding ends, most of these programs also end. Institutions need to bear responsibility for continuing to fund and administer successful access programs. Institutions also need to find ways to move away from numbers funding and look instead at impact. A program that supports less than 10% of the total student population should not be assessed funding based on numbers; rather, it should be funded based on community impact. As Nelson and Tachine (chapter 4) argue, as Native financial aid is an investment into the larger Native community, so too are access programs offered by colleges and universities.

Many researchers and communities call for decolonization. At a recent talk at Harvard University, Indigenous Australian curator Stephen Gilchrist (Yamatji People) stated, "Decolonizing is undoing. Indigenizing is doing." Many Western educational trends and policies should be undone, but many have significant use for tribal communities. Indigenizing these systems will necessarily require work that is done in different ways. How one tribal nation Indigenizes educational access may not be the same way another tribal nation addresses their needs. What is appropriate and necessary for one tribe will likely be different from another. Just as there is no single way to be Native, there is no single way to Indigenize, but overarching and guiding principles can allow each tribe to develop what works best.

We challenge institutions to move away from a one-model-fits-all way of thinking and take steps to explore their Native student community, surrounding Native community/communities, and local tribal culture. We also challenge our readers to think beyond access to college and the pipeline metaphor. Like the boarding schools that were forced on our people, pipelines have a negative connotation in Indian Country. Pipelines that carry fossil fuels, with the potential and a history of leaking toxic substances, have been forced on tribal communities and are symbols of continued colonization

(NYC Stands with Standing Rock Collective, 2016). Pitcher and Shahjahan (2017) discuss the limits of the pipeline metaphor in their article, using the metaphor of lemonade—mixing, tasting, and digesting—as a way to expand and challenge the unquestioned and normalized discourse of access to college. They argue against the pipeline metaphor, in that it dehumanizes students with its focus on the "pipeline as a conveyor of products" and an emphasis on "outcomes" and the degree "credential." The pipeline metaphor decontextualizes and depersonalizes the student experience, and it favors the pipeline. If students leak out of the pipeline, it is assumed a repair is needed, and the cost of repairs becomes the priority rather than examining the ingredients that make up the pipeline (e.g., school resources, college knowledge), how and what counts when those ingredients are mixed, and whether some pipes (institutions) digest (filter) only certain students through various educational processes.

Furthermore, the pipeline metaphor suggests a linear, fixed path to higher education. Our experience tells us that our students do not always follow a fixed path to college. Because of this reality, we choose to use the term *pathways* because it better represents the varied ways that Native students and communities are creating access to college. In the introduction, pathways were discussed as a way to conceptualize access to recognize the lived experiences of students. The moccasins on our cover are in a circle, representing the paths that lead back to nation building and community. We hope this book introduces and shares resources for Indigenizing access programs that honor our IKSs. Native students come into higher education with extremely unique and valuable experiences, understandings, and worldviews. An institution loses when this expertise is not engaged with, supported, and shared.

Conclusion

We wish to thank those who went before us; our communities; chapter authors; Stylus, in particular the patient John von Knorring; and Creator for making this book possible.

We are finished. Da•ne'thoh, and thank you, it is good: ahe'hee', ah-ho day-own-day, and nya weñha.

References

Almanac of Higher Education. (2016). *The chronicle of higher education.* Retrieved from www.chronicle.com/interactives/almanac-2016#id=7_132
Alaska Native Knowledge Network. (n.d.) *Alaska Native values for curriculum.* Retrieved from www.ankn.uaf.edu/ANCR/Values/

Bourdieu, P. (1986). The forms of capital. In J. G. Richardson (Ed.), *Handbook of theory and research for the sociology of education* (pp. 241–260). New York, NY: Greenwood Press.

College Links Outline. (2014). Unpublished report to Norman Board of Education, Norman Public Schools.

FCC Native Nations. (2017). *About the office.* Retrieved from www.fcc.gov/general/native-nations

Horse, P. (2001). Reflections on American Indian identity. In C. L. Wijeyesinghe & B. W. Jackson III (Eds.), *New perspectives on racial identity development: A theoretical and practical anthology* (pp. 91–107). New York, NY: New York University Press.

Huffman, T. (2001). Resistance theory and the transculturation hypothesis as explanations of college attrition and persistence among culturally traditional American Indian students. *Journal of American Indian Education, 40*(3), 1–23.

NYC Stands with Standing Rock Collective. (2016). *#StandingRockSyllabus.* Retrieved from https://nycstandswithstandingrock.wordpress.com/standingrocksyllabus/

Pitcher, E. N., & Shahjahan, R. A. (2017). From pipelines to tasting lemonade: Reconceptualizing college access. *Educational Studies, 53*(3), 216–232.

Ward, C. J. (2005). *Native Americans in the school system: Family, community and academic achievement.* Lanham, MD: AltaMira Press.

Waterman, S. J., & Lindley, L. (2013). Cultural strengths to persevere: American Indian women in higher education. *NASPA Journal About Women in Higher Education, 6*(2), 139–165.

Windchief, S., & Joseph, D. H. (2015). The act of claiming higher education as Indigenous space: American Indian/Alaska Native examples. *Diaspora, Indigenous, and Minority Education: Studies of Migration, Integration, Equity, and Cultural Survival, 9*(4), 267–283.

EDITORS AND CONTRIBUTORS

Monty Begaye (Diné) is a doctoral student in Adult and Higher Education at the University of Oklahoma.

LeManuel Lee Bitsói (Diné) is the chief diversity officer at State University New York, Stony Brook.

Jerry Bread (Kiowa/Cherokee) is the former community and outreach coordinator for Native American Studies at the University of Oklahoma.

Tina DeLapp is founder of the Recruitment and Retention of Alaska Natives into Nursing program and former director of the School of Nursing at the University of Alaska, Anchorage.

Susan C. Faircloth (Coharie Tribe of North Carolina) is professor of the Educational Leadership program at the University of North Carolina–Wilmington.

Breanna Faris (Cheyenne and Arapaho) is a doctoral student in adult and higher education at the University of Oklahoma and serves as the director of American Indian Student Life.

Nakay R. Flotte (Mescalero-Lipan Apache) is a doctoral candidate in the Department of Anthropology at Harvard University.

John L. Garland (Choctaw), PhD, is the director of Research and Student Success at Indigenous Education Incorporated, home of the Cobell Scholarship, and adjunct faculty for the College Student Development and Administration program at Shepherd University.

Adrienne Keene (Cherokee) is an assistant professor at Brown University and creator of the blog *Native Appropriations*.

163

Shelly C. Lowe (Diné) is the executive director of the Harvard University Native American Program.

George S. McClellan is a frequent coauthor and coeditor in student affairs and higher education and is grateful for the wonderful Native American scholar/practitioner friends and colleagues who enrich his learning and life.

Robin Minthorn (Kiowa/Nez Perce/Umatilla/Assiniboine) is assistant professor of educational leadership and Native American studies at the University of New Mexico.

Christine A. Nelson (Diné and Laguna Pueblo) is assistant professor of higher education at the University of Denver.

Jackie Pflaum is the program director for the Recruitment and Retention of Alaska Natives into Nursing program at the University of Alaska, Anchorage.

Stephanie Sanderlin (Yupik/Unangan) is a student success facilitator for the Recruitment and Retention of Alaska Natives into Nursing program at the University of Alaska, Anchorage.

David Sanders (Oglala Lakota) is the vice president for research, evaluation, and faculty development at the American Indian College Fund.

Heather J. Shotton (Wichita/Kiowa/Cheyenne) is associate professor of Native American studies at the University of Oklahoma.

Corey Still (Keetoowah Cherokee) is a doctoral student in adult and higher education at the University of Oklahoma.

Amanda R. Tachine (Diné) is a postdoctoral scholar in the Center for Indian Education at Arizona State University.

Luci Tapahonso (Diné) is the Inaugural Navajo Nation Poet Laureate.

Matthew Van Alstine Makomenaw (Grand Traverse Bay Band of Ottawa and Chippewa Indians) is the College Pathways administrator for the American Indian College Fund.

Stephanie J. Waterman (Onondaga) is associate professor of leadership, higher and adult education in the Ontario Institute for Studies in Education, the University of Toronto, and coordinates the student development, student services stream.

Natalie Rose Youngbull (Cheyenne and Arapaho/Assiniboine and Sioux) is the Faculty Fellowships program officer at the American Indian College Fund.

homesickness, 110–11
Horse, P., 160
Houtenville, A. J., 141–42, 145
Huffman, T., 35, 156

identities, 34–35, 42
IHS. *See* Indian Health Services
IKS. *See* Indigenous knowledge systems
income, 54, 82n1
Indian Adult Vocational Training Act, 71
Indian country, 6, 22
Indian Education Act, 122
Indian Education Student Services, 155, 157
Indian Health Services (IHS), 90, 143
Indian Self-Determination and Education Assistance Act, 72, 122–23, 132
Indigenized, 2
Indigenous, 2, 6. *See also* specific topics
Indigenous gaps, 10
Indigenous knowledge systems (IKS), 154
Indigenous scholars, 1
Individualized Education Plan, 144
ineligibility, 73
initiation, College Links, 155
institutional reports, 10
Institutional Research and Academic Career Development Award, 91
institutions, 22, 56–60
Integrated Postsecondary Education Data System (IPEDS), 56–57, 82n2
internships
  of higher education, 101–2
  of John, 43
  for Native education, 134
investment, government, 66, 71
IPEDS. *See* Integrated Postsecondary Education Data System

Jackson, A. P., 35
Jarsky, K. M., 1
job assistance, 113

John (pseudonym)
  bachelor degree completed by, 44
  college application by, 41–42
  family of, 40
  internships of, 43
  from Southwest tribe, 39
  stereotype of, 40
  student perspective of, 39–42
Johnson, D. R., 127, 135
Julliard, 99
Juris Doctorate, 48

Keetoowah Cherokee tribe, 117
Kennedy Report, 71, 72
Kin'yá'ání (Towering House clan), 47
Knorring, John von, 161
Kochhar-Bryant, C., 146
Kuslikis, A., 88–89

Lac Courte Oreilles Ojibwa Community College, 59
Lakota, 100
language, 55
large groups, 34
Laughlin, Whitney, 34
leadership, 129. *See also* Native education leadership program
  future generation of educational, 133–34
  in higher education, 126–28, 130–31
  in Native eduction leadership programs, 66, 124
  need for, 125–27
  Osah Gan Gio Model of, 127
  preparation for, 135
  programs for, 12
legislation, 143–44
Leitka, E., 125
lesbian, gay, bisexual, and transgender (LGBT), 83–84
LGBT. *See* lesbian, gay, bisexual, and transgender
LGBTQ community, 152
Lighting the Pathway program, 93

percentage all students in, 51
policies of, 74
research on, 60–61
role of, 127–28
staff of, 54–55
for STEM, 98–101
students of, 54–55
transfer rates of, 56–59
tuition cost of, 54
women of, 52
Tribal Leaders' Public Health
　Symposium, 97
Tribal Liaison, 48
Tribally Controlled Community
　College Act, 72, 73
Tribally Controlled Community
　College Assistance Act, 132
tribal nations
　control lacking in, 10
　financial aid and, 66
　identity for, 77
　involvement in, 71
　treaty agreements of, 70
Tribal Resources in Business,
　Engineering, and Science
　(TRIBES)
　closing of, 29
　college access of, 24–27
　cultural component of, 25–26
　educational opportunities of, 26–27
　financial aid of, 27
　residential experience for, 22, 24–26
TRIBES. *See* Tribal Resources in
　Business, Engineering, and Science
Tsui, L., 89–90
Tuba City High School, 47
tuition, 54
tutor coordinator and student success
　facilitators, 108–9
tutoring, 110

UA. *See* University of Arizona
UAA. *See* University of Alaska,
　Anchorage
undergraduates
　of AIGMS, 31
　college application for, 35
　disability of, 145
　enrollment of, 51
unemployment rates, 75–76
University of Alaska, Anchorage (UAA),
　108, 110, 113–14
　School of Nursing at, 111–12
University of Alaska Native Value, 111
University of Arizona (UA), 47, 131
University of Minnesota, 123
University of New Mexico (UNM), 22,
　96–97, 129, 131
University of Oklahoma (OU), 17, 47,
　94, 131, 155
　fraternity of, 119
　students at, 96, 157
University of Oregon, 131
UNM. *See* University of New Mexico

VanAlstine, M. J., 135
vocational training, 71–72, 143

Warner, L. S., 124–26, 127–28
Waterman, Stephanie J., 4–5
Weathers, R. R., 141–42
Wolverton, M., 35
women, 9, 52
Wright, B., 122, 132–33

Youngbull, Natalie
　of Arapahoe tribe, 21, 151
　of Assiniboine tribe, 21
　background of, 21–22, 30–31
　of Ft. Peck Sioux tribe, 21
　of Southern Cheyenne tribe, 21

At this juncture when the demographics of our schools and colleges are rapidly changing, critical mentoring provides mentors with a new and essential transformational practice that challenges deficit-based notions of protégés; questions their forced adaptation to dominant ideology; counters the marginalization and minoritization of young people of color; and endows them with voice, power, and choice to achieve in society while validating their culture and values.

Sty/us

22883 Quicksilver Drive
Sterling, VA 20166-2102

Subscribe to our e-mail alerts: www.Styluspub.com

Also available from Stylus

Beyond the Asterisk

Understanding Native Students in Higher Education

Edited by Heather J. Shotton, Shelly C. Lowe, and Stephanie J. Waterman

Foreword by John Garland

"Within this important and long overdue addition to the literature, higher education faculty and administrators have important new resources for helping shift the landscape of Native American college student experiences toward success. The importance of this particular new text cannot be understated. It has been conceived, written, and edited by Native American higher education leaders and those who have made Native students a priority in their practice. My hope is that this book becomes a catalyst for new higher education practices that lead to direct, and increased support for, Native Americans and others who are vigorously working to remove the Native American asterisk from research and practice. This text also signals a renewed call-to-action for increasing the representation of Native students, faculty, and staff on our campuses"—*John Garland*

The purpose of this book is to better understand Native students, challenge the status quo, and provide an informed base for leaders in student and academic affairs and administrators concerned with the success of students on their campuses. The contributors share their understanding of Native epistemologies, culture, and social structures, offering student affairs professionals and institutions a richer array of options, resources, and culturally relevant and inclusive models to better serve this population.

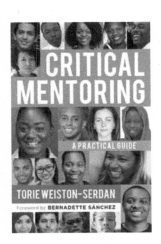

Critical Mentoring

A Practical Guide

Torie Weiston-Serdan

Foreword by Bernadette Sánchez

"*Critical Mentoring* is a savory blend of theories, thoughtful concepts, and evidence. Perhaps its practical utility is the book's most praiseworthy feature. Readers learn not only what this unique brand of mentoring is but also how to more effectively develop and support youth, particularly those who are often pushed to the margins."—*Shaun R. Harper, Professor and Executive Director, University of Pennsylvania Center for the Study of Race & Equity in Education*

(Continued on preceding page)